Key Stage 3
History for Wales

WALES
1000–1500

R. Paul Evans

Photo credits

Cover Caerphilly Castle © Adam Woolfitt/CORBIS; **p.4** *tl* © The Trustees of the British Museum, *tm* © The Art Archive/British Museum/Eileen Tweedy, *tr* © The National Archives/Heritage-Images/TopFoto, *b* Image courtesy of Archives and Special Collections, Bangor University; **p.5** *ml* Family life in the Iron Age (w/c on paper) by Birkbeck, Paul (20th Century) Private Collection/© English Heritage Photo Library/The Bridgeman Art Library, *tr* © Cadw, Welsh Assembly Government (Crown Copyright), *mr* Sir Thomas Mansel (1556-1631) and Jane (Pole) Lady Mansel (oil on canvas) by English School, (17th century) © National Museum Wales/The Bridgeman Art Library, *br* © Ceredigion Museum, Aberystwyth/Amgueddfa Ceredigion, Aberystwyth; **p.6** *tr* © The Photolibrary Wales/Alamy, *tl* © David Lyons/Alamy, *bl* © Paul Thompson Images/Alamy, *br* © R. Paul Evans; **p.7** *l* © Cadw, Welsh Assembly Government (Crown Copyright), *r* © Steve Preston; **p.14** *bl* © By permission of Llyfrgell Genedlaethol Cymru/The National Library of Wales, *tr* © Cadw, Welsh Assembly Government (Crown Copyright); **pp.14–15** © DC Photography – Fotolia; **p.18** © Cadw, Welsh Assembly Government (Crown Copyright); **p.19** © Cadw, Welsh Assembly Government (Crown Copyright); **p.25** © Cadw, Welsh Assembly Government (Crown Copyright); **p.27** © Cadw, Welsh Assembly Government (Crown Copyright); **p.29** *b* © Cadw, Welsh Assembly Government (Crown Copyright), *tl* © INTERFOTO/Alamy, *tr* © National Museum of Wales; **p.32** *br* © 2011 E&E Image Library/photolibrary.com, *tl* © National Museum of Wales; **p.37** © 2011 E&E Image Library/photolibrary.com; **p.38** © National Museum of Wales; **p.39** © Steve Preston; **p.40** © The British Library Board. All Rights reserved (Shelfmark Royal MS. 14C VII, f.136); **p.42** © The British Library Board. All Rights reserved (Shelfmark Cotton Vitellius MS A XIII, f.6v); **p.44** © Hulton Archive/Getty Images; **p.45** © Cadw, Welsh Assembly Government (Crown Copyright); **p.46** © The National Archives; **p.47** © Cadw, Welsh Assembly Government (Crown Copyright); **p.51** © 2010 Mary Evans Picture Library; **p.56** © The British Library Board. All Rights reserved (Shelfmark Royal 14 E. IV, f.23); **p.59** © Cadw, Welsh Assembly Government (Crown Copyright); **p.60** © The British Library Board. All Rights reserved (Shelfmark Royal 10 E. IV f.187); **p.62** © National Museum of Wales; **p.66** © A.F.Kersting/akg-images; **p.67** © Cadw, Welsh Assembly Government (Crown Copyright).

t = top, *b* = bottom, *l* = left, *r* = right, *m* = middle

Text acknowledgements

p.5 & p.55 *A Concise History of Wales*, Geraint H Jenkins, Cambridge University Press, 2007; **p.14** *Turning Points in Welsh History 1485–1914*, Stuart Broomfield and Euryn Madoc-Jones, University of Wales Press, 2004; **p.13** *Stories from Welsh History*, H T Evans, The Educational Publishing Company, 1935; **p.18** *The History of Wales*, G P Ambrose, E J Arnold & Son, 1947; **p.23, p.54 & p.57** *Medieval Wales*, A D Carr, Palgrave Macmillan, 1995; **p.31** *Looking at Welsh History*, A J Roderick, A & C Black, 1968; **p.35** *Gwenllian: The Welsh Warrior Princess*, Peter Newton, Gwasg Carreg Gwalch 2002; **p.45** *Wales in the Middle Ages*, Catrin Stevens, Oxford University Press, 1992; **p.49 & p.63** source 4 *A Short History of Modern Wales*, David Williams, John Murray, 1951; **p.63** source 5 www.bbc.co.uk/wales/history/sites/themes/figures/owain_glyndwr.shtml; **p.64** Henry Tudor and Wales, Glanmor Williams, Gwasg Prifysgol Cymru, 1985; **p.65** *Modern Welsh History*, Idris Jones, G Bell & Sons, 1960.

Words in **bold** are defined in the glossary on page 69.

Orders: please contact Bookpoint Ltd, 130 Milton Park, Abingdon, Oxon OX14 4SB. Telephone: +44 (0)1235 827720. Fax: +44 (0)1235 400454. Lines are open 9.00a.m.–5.00p.m., Monday to Saturday, with a 24-hour message answering service. Visit our website at www.hoddereducation.co.uk.

© R. Paul Evans 2011

First published in 2011 by
Hodder Education,
an Hachette UK company
338 Euston Road
London NW1 3BH

Impression number   10 9 8 7 6 5 4 3 2 1
Year   2015 2014 2013 2012 2011

Typeset in Palatino 12/14pt
Layouts designed by Lorraine Inglis Design
Artwork by Barking Dog Art, Richard Duszczak, Janek Matysiak and Tony Randell
Printed and bound in Italy

A catalogue record for this title is available from the British Library

ISBN 978 1 444 13359 2

contents

Introduction to the study of history at Key Stage 3

In this section you will learn how to:
- ➲ **identify** the skills used by historians
- ➲ **understand** how historians use these skills to investigate the past
- ➲ **apply** those skills through the undertaking of an historical enquiry.

Did you know?
The word 'history' comes from the Greek word *historeo*, which means to enquire about something.

1.1 What is history and how is it studied?

History is the study of events that have happened in the past and the people who have lived through those events. History is about enquiry, asking questions about the past, and the people who study history are called historians.

History is about …

a ... finding out about the past.

b ... asking questions about evidence.

c ... working out why things happened.

k ... understanding how and why viewpoints have been formed.

j ... developing and supporting an argument.

d ... putting things into their correct order of time.

e ... recording information.

i ... constructing a narrative (story) of what happens.

h ... using different sources of information.

g ... deciding what was important in the past and why.

f ... writing down dates and facts.

ACTIVITY

You are going to answer the question, 'What is history about?'

a) Think about the statements a to k on this page. Which ones do you agree with most?

b) Rank the statements to show which you think best describes what history is about. The best description should come first.

c) Compare your list with a partner. If there are differences, agree on a new list together.

d) Share your ideas with the rest of the class and say which statements you feel best describe what history is about, and why.

e) How else might you describe what history is about? Use your previous experience of history lessons or general knowledge.

1.2 How do historians investigate the past?

To uncover the past historians operate like detectives, searching for clues or **evidence** that the past has left behind. They have to interpret those clues to work out the order in which things occurred, and to work out their causes and their consequences. To do this, historians have to carry out investigations. During the investigations they have to ask a series of questions:

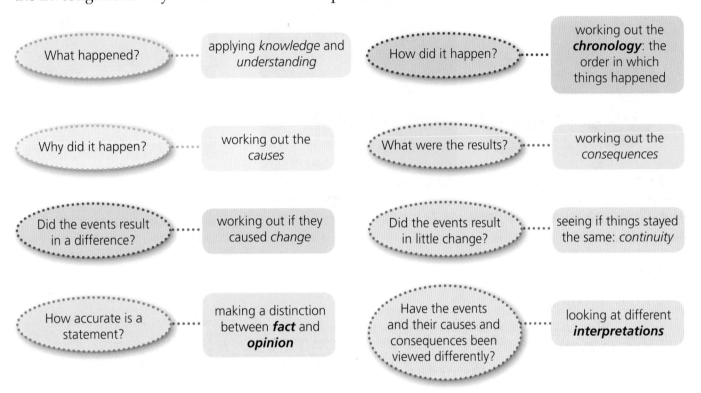

What happened? ······ applying *knowledge* and *understanding*

How did it happen? ······ working out the **chronology**: the order in which things happened

Why did it happen? ······ working out the *causes*

What were the results? ······ working out the *consequences*

Did the events result in a difference? ······ working out if they caused *change*

Did the events result in little change? ······ seeing if things stayed the same: *continuity*

How accurate is a statement? ······ making a distinction between **fact** and **opinion**

Have the events and their causes and consequences been viewed differently? ······ looking at different *interpretations*

The skills a historian needs

Looking for evidence

Understanding the type of evidence

Understanding problems with the evidence

Dating the evidence

Reaching a conclusion

Like a detective investigating the scene of a crime, the historian will need to use a variety of skills to uncover the sequence of events, and the causes and consequences of the events, in order to answer the questions above.

1 Looking for evidence: Research

The first task of the historian is to look for the clues or evidence which the past has left behind. This evidence can include:

Physical objects

▲ Cooking pots and metal tools dating from the Iron Age

Source **2**

Visual objects

▲ A photograph of a coalminer in the South Wales valleys having a bath after his shift down the pit has ended. It is dated around 1920

Source **3**

Written accounts

August 1st the Wind W. in the morning, calm sun shining & fair, about 9 it came to S. blew fresh, grew dark with some rain about 11, but about 1 it began in earnest to rain, and rained hard all the rest of the day & blowing high besides: My people were forced to leave the hay, & go to fence the wet ditch in the field behind Jerem house: I sowed to day Cauly Flower, Cabbage & Onion Seeds.

◀ An extract from the diary of William Bulkeley of Brynddu, Anglesey. Bulkeley kept a diary from 1734 to 1760. It records details of the social life, customs and traditions, political events and the weather on Anglesey in the middle years of the eighteenth century

ACTIVITIES

1 Study the table on the right, which contains examples of the different types of evidence used by historians.

  a) In pairs, decide which can be classed as (i) physical objects, (ii) visual objects and (iii) written pieces of evidence

  b) Compare your answers with others in the class. Are they the same? If not, discuss why you disagree.

2 Study Source 1. What does it tell you about life in the Iron Age?

3 Source 2 is a photograph of working class life in the 1920s. What would you include in a photograph to show historians of the future what a living room of today looks like?

4 Source 3 is an extract from a diary written in the eighteenth century. Think of three reasons why diaries can be useful pieces of evidence to the historian.

A: Pottery	B: Newspapers	C: Tapestries
D: Letters	E: Coins	F: Skeleton
G: Ruins	H: History books	I: Weapons
J: Photographs	K: Films	L: Documents

2 Understanding the type of evidence: Analysis and evaluation

Historians call different examples of evidence **sources**. These sources can be divided into two types:

> **primary evidence** (or *contemporary* evidence which dates from that time period)

> **secondary evidence** (or *reflective* evidence which was produced after the time period).

Both types of evidence are useful to historians but, as we shall see later in this skills section, they have to be treated with care.

On this page are five examples of primary and secondary evidence (Sources 4–8). Study each of them carefully.

Source 5

◄ An artist's impression of the inside of an Iron Age roundhouse

Source 4

▲ Reconstruction of the great chamber in the Elizabethan town house of Plas Mawr in Conwy, as it would have appeared in the late Tudor period

Source 6

▲ Portrait of Sir Thomas Mansel of Margam and his wife painted in the 1590s

Source 7

For most people in the South Wales valleys life was a daily battle against poverty, disease and death ... When the coal rush began long rows of small terraced houses were built along the valley slopes ... poor sanitation and poor diets encouraged the spread of infectious diseases such as tuberculosis [TB] and cholera.

A description of living conditions in the mining towns of South Wales in the late nineteenth century. The extract is from *A Concise History of Wales*, a history textbook by Geraint H. Jenkins (2007)

Source 8

▲ A photograph, taken in 1882, of an old lady standing outside her cottage in Cardiganshire

ACTIVITIES

1 Identify which of Sources 4–8 are primary and which are secondary pieces of evidence. Give a reason for each decision.

2 Study each of the sources more closely, thinking about their strengths and weaknesses as pieces of historical evidence. Copy and complete the table below – Source 6 has been done for you.

Source	Strengths	Weaknesses
6	Dating from the time of Elizabeth I, the painting is a good example of the clothes worn by the rich during the Tudor period.	A painting is not like a photograph – we do not know if it is a true likeness of Sir Thomas Mansel and his wife.

3 Dating the evidence: Chronology

An important part of inspecting a source is to date the evidence, placing items into their correct order in time. This will enable the source to be placed in a sequence of events, showing what came before and what came after. It is also important to be able to date things and events to particular historical periods, and to recognise the characteristics of different periods.

ACTIVITIES

1 Work out the correct century that each of the following dates fits into:
   987; 1349; 1666; 1851; 2000.

2 a) Think about five important events in your life. Record them on a timeline similar to the one below:

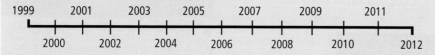

b) What evidence do you have for these events?

3 The following six sources (9–14) show housing from different time periods. Study them carefully. What have you already learnt about these buildings from previous history lessons?

Key terms used by historians to record time

Decade	10 years
Century	100 years
Millennium	1000 years
BC	Before Christ
AD	Anno Domini (*The year of our Lord*)

Placing a year into its correct century

Eleventh	1000–1099
Twelfth	1100–1199
Thirteenth	1200–1299
Fourteenth	1300–1399
Fifteenth	1400–1499

Source 9

Source 10

Source 11

Source 12

Descriptive labels of each building

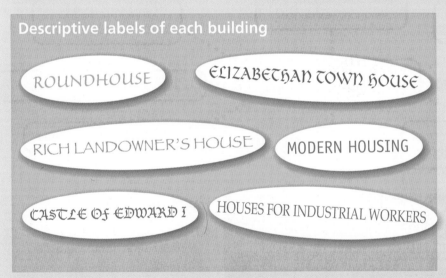

ROUNDHOUSE

ELIZABETHAN TOWN HOUSE

RICH LANDOWNER'S HOUSE

MODERN HOUSING

CASTLE OF EDWARD I

HOUSES FOR INDUSTRIAL WORKERS

4 Working in pairs:

a) Match the descriptive labels (left) to each of the sources 9–14.

b) Write a description of each building saying how it is used.

c) List the buildings in their correct chronological order, starting with the oldest building.

d) Match a historical time period (below) to each building label.

e) Can you suggest reasons why the buildings are different?

Compare your results with others in the class. Are they the same?

Historical time periods

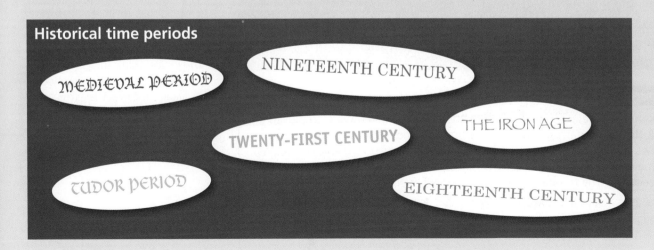

NINETEENTH CENTURY

MEDIEVAL PERIOD

THE IRON AGE

TWENTY-FIRST CENTURY

TUDOR PERIOD

EIGHTEENTH CENTURY

4 Understanding problems with the evidence: Interpretation

The historian will need to ask questions to check if the evidence is useful and also whether it is reliable or not. Evidence can be viewed in different ways, and the opinions historians hold may be affected by: their particular views or attitudes; the type of audience they are writing for; the reasons why they are writing; and by the circumstances under which they are writing. People often have differing opinions about events, their causes and consequences.

The evidence can be fact or opinion. If it is opinion then it could be one-sided or **biased**. An example of one-sided opinion can be seen in Source 15.

To find out whether a source is primary or secondary and whether it is fact or opinion, historians must consider the usefulness and reliability of the evidence. In order to do this they need to ask a series of questions about the evidence.

> **Source 15**
>
> It is the habit of the Welsh to steal anything they can lay their hands on and to live on plunder, theft and robbery, not only from foreigners and people hostile to them, but also from each other … They think more of material gain, however shameful, than they do of the need to keep a promise or observe an oath.
>
> This is an account about the honesty of the Welsh. It was written in the 1190s by the monk Gerald of Wales in his book *A Description of Wales*.

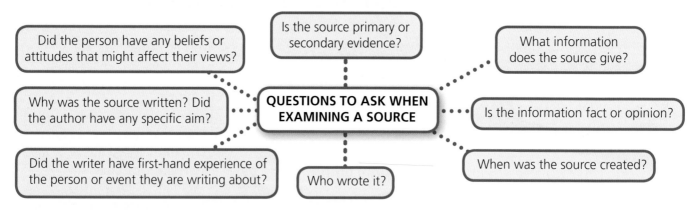

- Did the person have any beliefs or attitudes that might affect their views?
- Is the source primary or secondary evidence?
- What information does the source give?
- Why was the source written? Did the author have any specific aim?
- **QUESTIONS TO ASK WHEN EXAMINING A SOURCE**
- Is the information fact or opinion?
- Did the writer have first-hand experience of the person or event they are writing about?
- Who wrote it?
- When was the source created?

Gerald of Wales (*Giraldus Cambrensis*), 1146–1223

Much of our knowledge of Welsh history for the period 1000 to 1500 comes from the writings of medieval monks such as Gerald of Wales. In 1188 he accompanied Baldwin, the archbishop of Canterbury, on a tour to recruit Welsh soldiers to fight in the Third Crusade. As a result of this journey he wrote two books:

- *An Itinerary of Wales* (1191) which described his journey, and
- *A Description of Wales* (1194) which dealt with the geography of Wales and the everyday life of the Welsh people.

> **Source 16**
>
> During the nineteenth century, large numbers of children were employed in industry, doing dangerous work. The opening and closing of doors in the mines was always done by children. The damp, dirty, unhygienic conditions, combined with working in total darkness, would reduce their life expectancy. The trappers, as they were called, were coffin fodder!
>
> Historians Stuart Broomfield and Euryn Madoc-Jones are describing working conditions for children in their school history textbook, *Turning Points in Welsh History 1485–1914* (2004)

ACTIVITIES

1 Read Source 15 and the information about Gerald of Wales.

   a) Which parts of the quotation in Source 15 do you think are opinion and which parts are fact?

   b) Do you think this source is of any use to the historian studying life in medieval Wales? Give reasons for your answer.

2 Examine Source 16 using the questions from the diagram above.

5 Reaching a conclusion: Judgement

The final stage in investigating the past is for the historian to weigh up all the evidence and apply his or her own investigative skills to reach a conclusion about what happened in the past, why it happened and what its results were.

The processes adopted by a historian to investigate the past

Searching for evidence

↓

Understanding the type of evidence

↓

Arranging the evidence into its order of time

↓

Understanding any problems with the evidence

↓

Reaching a conclusion based upon the evidence

ACTIVITIES

1 You have been asked by an American TV company to provide them with information on what life was like for people living in Britain during three different time periods:

- a farmer living in the Iron Age
- a rich family living in the Tudor Age
- a working class family living in the nineteenth century.

Look back over pages 4–8 and select those sources that will help you in your enquiry. Copy and complete the chart below with your findings.

What the evidence tells me	A farmer living in the Iron Age	A rich family living in the Tudor Age	A working class family living in the nineteenth century
Type of house they lived in:	*(in this space you should name the source you have used and say what it tells you)*		
Types of clothes they wore:			
Types of furniture in their house:			
Their lifestyle:			
Why have you selected this type of evidence?			
What other types of evidence should be examined?			

2 Think about how historians of the future will find out about what life was like in the early twenty-first century.

a) In pairs, make a list of six pieces of evidence that would help future historians find out what your life was like. Study this cartoon for some clues about what to include in your list.

b) Write a paragraph about your six pieces of evidence, explaining to the historian of the future why these sources would be useful.

c) Compare your list with others in your class. How do the lists differ?

1.3 Introducing your 'History Skills' friends

At the end of Key Stage 3 you will be assessed upon your ability to perform in five skills areas.

Let me introduce you to your 'History Skills' friends; these friends will be with you throughout your course. Each time you see one of the icons below you will know which friend will be helping you and what skills you will be using. You can find the icons at the top of each section opening page and on each end of section assessment page.

 Father Time – chronological awareness

I put things in order of time.

I am able to compare one time period with another.

It is important to understand the order in which things happened.

My knowledge will help me to date things to a particular period of time.

 Professor Know-All – historical knowledge and understanding

I can remember historical details and use my knowledge to understand things.

I can describe the key features of a particular period.

I can use my knowledge to work out why things happened, why they happened in the way they did, what effects such things had, and whether the effects caused change or resulted in things staying the same.

 Dr Two-Sides – interpretations of history

I will help you to consider whether there is more than one side to a story.

Historians will come up with differing opinions.

I know that history is always open to interpretation; people and events will be viewed in different ways.

 Inspector Q – historical enquiry

I will help you to consider the evidence very carefully to discover the characteristics of a particular period.

I will help you to record and evaluate information, and reach a reasoned conclusion.

I must ask questions about the evidence to find out when it dates from, what it tells us and what its purpose was.

Ms Perfect – organisation and communication

I will help to produce narratives and descriptions; to explain and to reason.

I will help you to use appropriate historical terminology.

I will provide structure to your work, making full use of sentences, paragraphs and punctuation.

1.4 Your journey through history at Key Stage 3

You are about to begin your journey through Key Stage 3 history. Along the route you will be able to practise and develop your historical skills.

It is important that you check your progress at regular intervals. This will enable you to:

> reflect upon what you have achieved

> work out what you need to do to improve and develop your performance in the various history skills.

ACTIVITIES

1 Make a copy of the following History Skills wall in your book.
   a) Put a green dot beside the skills you know how to use.
   b) Put an amber dot beside the skills you need to practise more.
   c) Put a red dot beside the skills you have not yet developed.
2 As you come to the end of each section of this book, repeat question 1 to show how your skills have progressed.

Checking evidence before believing what I see and read.	Understanding what an interpretation is.	Comparing and contrasting different types of interpretations.	Identify why some historical interpretations are more valid than others.
	Deciding which points are relevant to a particular argument.	Drawing up criteria to decide the significance of certain events and people.	Prioritising changes from the most to the least important.	
Show an awareness of chronology and differing timeframes.	Giving several reasons for an event happening, not just one.	Classifying changes into long and short term and their consequences.	Assessing how relevant an important event from the past still is today.
	Make links between people, events and changes within and across periods.	Recognise the characteristic features of a period, situation or society.	Use specialist vocabulary to describe historical periods and the passage of time.	
	Demonstrate the ability to use a range of historical sources.		Record and evaluate information, and reach a reasoned conclusion.

End of section assessment: Understanding history at Key Stage 3

In this section you have found out what the study of history is all about. You have been introduced to the five skills used by historians to help them investigate the past. You are now going to apply this knowledge to develop your history skills to solve a murder mystery.

It is 7a.m. on Saturday, 9 June 2010. You are a detective in the South Wales police who has been called to investigate an unexplained death. The body of a man dressed in a dinner suit has been found in a ditch just outside Mystery Manor, an isolated property some way outside Cardiff. It is the home of billionaire Mr Henry Host, the owner of a major drug manufacturing company.

The body displays injuries to the head, giving the appearance of having been hit with a heavy object. There are no signs of injury to any other parts of the body. In the suit pockets these nine items were found:

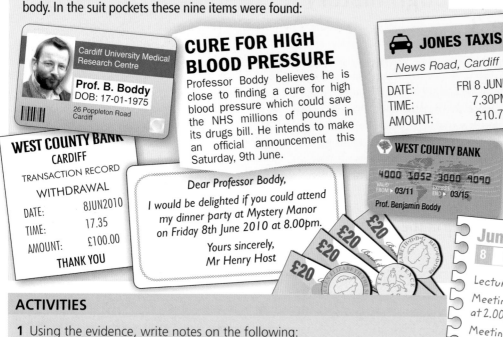

ACTIVITIES

1 Using the evidence, write notes on the following:
- what you know about the dead person
- the possible movements of that person
- who you would like to interview and what questions you would ask.

2 Having completed your investigation you now need to write up your final report using the following factors to consider:
- Who is the dead person?
- How did his body end up outside Mystery Manor?
- When do you think this incident took place?
- Who is the main suspect?
- Have you found any evidence to link this person to the crime?
- Have you got enough evidence to charge the suspect and to take the case to court?

3 Compare your report with others in the class. How do they differ? Can you suggest reasons why you and your friends may have reached different conclusions?

Through this exercise you will have developed an understanding of how and why historians can reach different conclusions on the basis of studying the same evidence.

Was the coming of the Normans a 'turning point' in Welsh history?

In this section you will learn how to:

➲ **ask questions** about how and why Wales was affected by the arrival of the Normans

➲ **understand** what changed and what stayed the same

➲ **make judgements** about the extent of these changes.

Turning Point – A turning point is an event or development in history which has resulted in a major change. For example, in recent times the attack on the Twin Towers in New York in September 2001 by members of Al-Qaeda resulted in America launching a 'war on terror'. This led to the invasions of Afghanistan and Iraq. A single event caused a major shift in international relations.

In this section you will investigate whether the coming of the Normans changed Wales. In order to complete this investigation you will need to consider the following:

❯ what Wales was like before 1066

❯ why and how the Normans began to push into Wales

❯ the reaction of the native Welsh rulers to this invasion of their lands

❯ who the Marcher lords were and how they ruled

❯ the changes introduced by the new Norman rulers.

By the end of this investigation you will be able to make a judgement on whether these changes meant that the coming of the Normans was a 'turning point' in the history of Wales.

ACTIVITY

What does Source 1 tell you about the Norman advance into Wales?

PLANNING YOUR INVESTIGATION

Before you begin your investigation think about the questions you will need to ask to find out about these changes and their impact upon life in Wales. To help prepare yourself for this, copy and fill in the table below.

Wales and the coming of the Normans	
Three things I already know about Wales and the Normans:	**Three questions** I want to ask to help me in my investigation:

Source 1

The Normans conquered England in 1066 by means of their army led by King William, but the conquest of Wales was gradual. It was brought about by Norman barons who, by building strong castles, slowly brought the surrounding country under their power.

H. T. Evans, *Stories from Welsh History*, 1935

2.1 What was Wales like before 1066?

In this topic you are going to investigate what Wales was like before 1066: how it was ruled, how people lived and how it compared to England.

Source **1**

Unlike England which was one kingdom, Wales was divided into a number of kingdoms, the most important being:

- Gwynedd in the north
- Powys in mid-Wales
- Deheubarth in the south.

There were also the smaller kingdoms of Gwent, Morgannwg and Brycheiniog. The border which separated Wales from England was a dyke built by Offa, King of Mercia, in the eighth century to stop the Welsh attacking his lands.

Before the arrival of the Normans, Christianity had been spread by missionaries such as St David, St Beuno and St Teilo. This led to the development of the Welsh Church from the Celtic religion. There were churches in every settlement; these were led by priests. Bishops had no cathedrals. They controlled **dioceses** which mirrored the lands of the various kingdoms and so changed as they did.

◀ Carew Cross in Pembrokeshire with its Celtic design. It commemorates Maredudd ab Edwin, the king of Deheubarth who died in 1035

Each kingdom was ruled over by its own king or prince. The kingdoms were often at war with each other. Between 949AD and the Norman attacks on Wales in the 1070s over 25 kings were killed in battle. England was ruled by one king, Harold II, who became king after the death of Edward the Confessor in January 1066.

The illustration shows Hywel Dda (Hywel the Good), King of Deheubarth, who died in 949. He managed to spread his rule over large parts of Wales.

▲ Hywel the Good shown in his role as lawmaker and judge

What was Wales like before 1066?

Wales was a land of high mountains and deep valleys. Travel was difficult and slow, especially in the mountains of Gwynedd. This made it hard for any one ruler to gain control over the whole of Wales, but it also made it very difficult for invaders from outside Wales to conquer Welsh lands. The Welsh could always retreat to the mountains and aim to ambush the invading forces in the narrow mountain passes or in the dense forests which filled the valley bottoms. The flatter land of England made travel and the movement of armies much easier.

There were few towns in Wales. Most of the dwelling places were scattered farms, and were not clustered around the local church as in English villages and towns.

Each king or prince lived in his own palace, called a **Llys**, which was most often made of wood with a thatched roof, although sometimes it was built of stone. The Llys was made up of a central hall, a chapel, stables and storehouses, and was surrounded by a timber wall and sometimes a ditch. Here the ruler feasted with his officers and was entertained by his chief **bard** who composed poems in his honour.

The king of England would reside in more substantial buildings and would be surrounded by a larger court. The king would spend his time journeying around the country, from one royal palace to another.

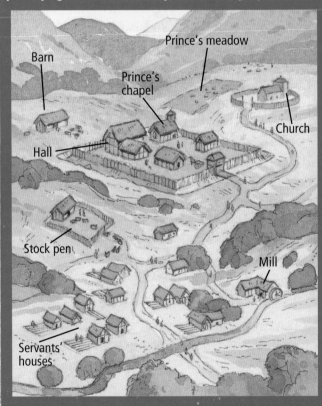

Barn

Prince's chapel

Prince's meadow

Church

Hall

Stock pen

Mill

Servants' houses

◀ An artist's impression of the Llys of a Welsh prince

Under Welsh law every male had a right to inherit land from his father, unlike in England where only the oldest son would inherit all the estate. This meant that over time Welsh estates got smaller and smaller.

Welsh people lived simply. Their food was meat, milk, cheese, butter and bread. They ate more meat than bread, because they were cattle farmers rather than crop growers. The English grew crops, such as wheat and oats, so frequently ate bread and porridge, as well as vegetables, meat, fish and dairy products.

Source 2

It is two hundred miles long and about one hundred miles wide. It takes some eight days to travel the whole length from the mouth of the River Gwygir in Anglesey to Portskewett in Gwent … Its high mountains, deep valleys and large forests, its rivers and marshes, make travelling across Wales very difficult.

From *A Description of Wales* by the monk Gerald of Wales, 1194

ACTIVITIES

1 What does Source 2 tell you about the problems facing any invasion force planning to attack Wales?

2 Using Source 1, describe what Wales was like before 1066. In your answer you should refer to:

   a) how it was ruled
   b) how the people lived
   c) why it was difficult to conquer.

3 Work together in pairs to copy and complete the table below, using Source 1.

What were the differences between Wales and England before 1066?	
Wales	England

Extension task

4 Did the differences between Wales and England before 1066 make it harder for invaders to attack and conquer Wales? Give reasons for your answer.

2.2 **Why did the Normans take so long to push into Wales?**

In this topic you are going to investigate the reasons why the Normans took so long to advance into Wales. Was it because the king was too busy in England fighting off rebellions to advance into Wales himself, and instead sent the Norman barons to defend his borders? Was it because the Norman barons didn't work together, each fighting individual battles with the Welsh forces? Was it because of the strong resistance from the Welsh to the Norman advances? Or was it because the geography of Wales made it so difficult to conquer?

ACTIVITY

1 Copy the living graph below. When you read about an event on pages 16–17, add a note about it on the graph, placing it either higher up to show it was good for the Norman barons, or lower to show it was good for the Welsh. In this way you will record the first phase of the Norman penetration into Wales between 1066 and 1100.

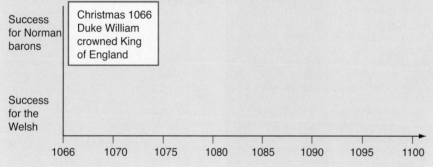

Success for Norman barons

Christmas 1066 Duke William crowned King of England

Success for the Welsh

1066   1070   1075   1080   1085   1090   1095   1100

Background
The year 1066 was a turning point in the history of England. In October the Saxon King Harold II was defeated and killed at the Battle of Hastings by the Frenchman, Duke William of Normandy. As a result of that battle, William now claimed control of England and he became its first Norman ruler, King William I, or the Conqueror. One battle had changed the course of English history.

◄ **Hugh of Avranches** ('Hugh the Fat') was created Earl of Chester

▶ **Roger of Montgomery** was created Earl of Shrewsbury

◄ **William Fitzosbern** (William's cousin) was created Earl of Hereford

How the Norman barons first pushed into Wales

In the years immediately after 1066, William the Conqueror was too busy putting down rebellions across England to try to push Norman rule into Wales. Instead, he decided to protect his border with Wales by creating three **earldoms** and he appointed three of his most trusted Norman barons to rule there in his name: Hugh of Avranches, Roger of Montgomery and William Fitzosbern (see right).

These barons were given permission by King William to cross the border of Offa's Dyke and attack the Welsh kingdoms. Any land they conquered could be ruled by them in the name of the king. By 1136 they had extended Norman rule deep into areas of Wales but they had not conquered the whole of Wales.

The Norman advances into north Wales

In 1070 Hugh, Earl of Chester, together with his cousin, Robert of Rhuddlan, began their advance along the north Wales coast from their fortress at Chester.

In 1073 Robert built a **motte and bailey** castle at Rhuddlan (see Source 2, page 18) to guard the crossing of the river Clwyd and in the following years he pushed into Gwynedd, building another castle at Degannwy to mark the edge of his territory at the river Conwy.

(see Source 2, page 18)

ACTIVITY

2 Look at your completed living graph (see page 16). What does it tell you about the first phase of the Norman penetration into Wales? Are there more successes for the Normans or for the Welsh? Does this change over time?

(see page 16)

Source **1**

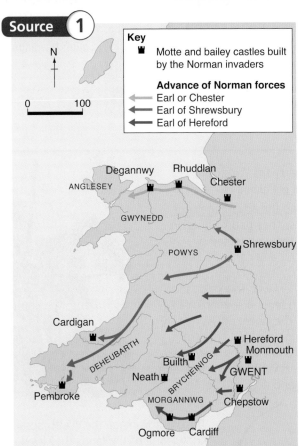

Key

🏰 Motte and bailey castles built by the Norman invaders

Advance of Norman forces
← Earl or Chester
← Earl of Shrewsbury
← Earl of Hereford

0   100

N

Degannwy   Rhuddlan
ANGLESEY   Chester

GWYNEDD

POWYS   Shrewsbury

Cardigan

DEHEUBARTH

Hereford
Monmouth
Builth
BRYCHEINIOG
Neath   GWENT
MORGANNWG   Chepstow
Pembroke

Ogmore   Cardiff

◀ Map showing the Norman advances into Wales

The Norman push into mid-Wales

In 1071 Roger, Earl of Shrewsbury, marched along the Severn valley and crossed the mountain ranges of mid-Wales to the coast at Ceredigion, securing his conquests by building a castle at Cardigan.

During the 1090s Hugh the Proud, the son of Earl Roger of Shrewsbury, advanced south as far as Pembroke where he built another strong castle.

The Norman push into south Wales

In 1067 William Fitzosbern, Earl of Hereford, advanced across the Welsh border and captured lands in the kingdoms of Gwent and Brycheiniog. To protect his new possessions he built castles at Monmouth and Chepstow (see Source 6, page 19) but the surrounding hills remained in Welsh hands. Resistance by Rhys ap Tewdwr, Prince of Deheubarth, blocked their advances but after his death the Normans made rapid progress into the rest of south Wales.

(see Source 6, page 19)

During the 1090s Bernard of Neufmarché extended Norman rule over the rest of Brycheiniog, while Philip de Braose moved into Radnor.

Robert Fitzhamon, Earl of Gloucester, captured the kingdom of Morgannwg and built castles at Cardiff, Neath and Ogmore, creating the lordship of Glamorgan.

Source 2

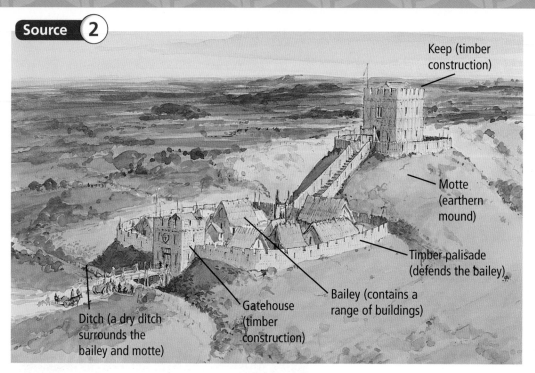

Keep (timber construction)

Motte (earthern mound)

Timber palisade (defends the bailey)

Bailey (contains a range of buildings)

Gatehouse (timber construction)

Ditch (a dry ditch surrounds the bailey and motte)

◀ The motte and bailey castle built at Rhuddlan by Robert in 1073. The motte was a large earthen mound upon which was built a wooden tower or **keep**. Below this was an area of flat land, the bailey, which was surrounded by a timber **palisade** and a deep ditch. Within the bailey were living quarters for the knights and soldiers, stables for their horses, workshops for the blacksmith, food stores and other buildings.

Source 3

It was in south Wales that the Normans had most success. Advancing along the fertile coastal plain and the great river valleys of Severn, Wye and Usk, the Norman knights set themselves up as great lords or barons. They built castles at Chepstow, Monmouth, Cardiff, Pembroke and other places to secure their conquests.

G. P. Ambrose, *The History of Wales*, 1947

Source 4

In north Wales the land was harder to conquer, for the coastal plain was narrow and fringed with forests from which the Welsh could make sudden attacks. For a time it looked as though Anglesey would be conquered but the advance of Hugh the Fat was stopped. The limit of their power was the castles of Rhuddlan and Degannwy. Even these were sometimes taken by the Welsh. In the mountain stronghold of Snowdonia, the princes of Gwynedd held their own against the invaders.

G. P. Ambrose, *The History of Wales*, 1947

Source 5

Differences between the Welsh and Norman methods of fighting

The Normans had the advantage over the Welsh forces. They had knights on horseback who were protected by chain-mail armour and carried a lance, sword and shield. These knights were protected by archers who fought on foot.

The Welsh had few horses and mainly fought on foot. They were not as heavily protected, having only light coats of chain-mail, swords and lances. They relied upon their archers who had a reputation for being fierce and accurate fighters.

The one advantage the Welsh possessed was knowledge of the lands they lived in. They avoided large **pitched battles** in favour of small surprise attacks, operating as guerrilla fighters do today. They took the enemy by surprise and then quickly disappeared into the surrounding lands, leaving the Norman enemy stunned and unable to fight back. However, they were unable to stop the Normans from building motte and bailey castles which they used as bases for their soldiers to attack the surrounding countryside.

ACTIVITIES

3 Copy and complete the table below using the information and sources on pages 16–19 and your own knowledge.

	North Wales	Mid-Wales	South Wales
Name of Norman lord leading the attack			
Year of first attack			
Details of castles built			
Norman success or failure?			

4 Study Sources 3 and 4. Which regions of Wales resisted the Norman advances best – the north or south? Suggest reasons for your answer.

5 Study the information and pictures in Source 5.

   a) Identify three differences between Welsh and Norman forces and their methods of fighting.

   b) Explain why the Welsh method of avoiding large battles made it difficult to defeat them.

   c) How did the building of motte and bailey castles help the Normans to achieve control over areas of Wales?

Extension task

6 In pairs, compile a list of reasons why you think the Normans were unable to gain control of Wales in a single battle as they had gained control of England at the Battle of Hastings.

REVIEWING YOUR INVESTIGATION

a) How many of the questions you asked at the start of this investigation (see page 13) have now been answered?

b) Think of some other questions that you would now like to ask to further your investigation.

Source (6)

◀ The Great Tower at Chepstow castle built by William Fitzosbern between 1067–71. It was one of the first Norman castles in Britain to be built of stone. It shows how strong the Welsh resistance must have been.

Strong Welsh resistance to the first phase of Norman attacks

As we have seen, the first advances of the Normans into Wales involved the forces of the Earls of Hereford, Shrewsbury and Chester, but they did not combine and fight as one force. This proved to be a major weakness as it allowed the Welsh rulers to fight each force separately.

The Norman advance into Wales took place over many decades. During that time they faced constant rebellions from the native Welsh rulers. On several occasions, the Normans were pushed back from the areas they thought they had conquered. Two Welsh princes attempted to resist the first phase of the Norman advance in the 1090s: the prince of Deheubarth, Rhys ap Tewdwr, and the prince of Gwynedd, Gruffudd ap Cynan.

The story of the prince of Deheubarth: Rhys ap Tewdwr

In 1078, Rhys ap Tewdwr's cousin died in battle. Rhys then became the prince of Deheubarth.

However, in 1081 a rival Welsh prince wanted his throne. Rhys was forced to join forces with Gruffudd ap Cynan, ruler of Gwynedd, in order to defend his throne and defeat the rival prince.

Later that year, King William came to Wales from England; it was his only visit. He came along the south coast to St David's, where he met with Rhys. They made an agreement together which brought peace to Rhys' region for the next six years.

When King William died in 1087, there was a new king of England called William Rufus. He encouraged the Norman barons to push further into Wales, to attack and conquer land still under Welsh control. Rhys again had to defend his lands. To do this, he joined forces with the prince of the neighbouring kingdom, Brycheiniog.

In April 1093 Rhys was in Brycheiniog, attempting to resist the Normans invading the kingdom near the new Norman castle at Brecon. He was killed during the battle.

Rhys ap Tewdwr did much to bring peace to south-west Wales. However, after he died, there were many more attacks on this region. By 1136, the Normans were in firm control of south-west Wales.

ACTIVITIES

1 Who was more successful in resisting Norman rule – Rhys ap Tewdwr or Gruffudd ap Cynan? Remember to give reasons for your answer.

2 Study illustration 5 on page 21 showing the surprise attack on Robert of Rhuddlan's castle and Source 7.

   a) Which source is primary and which is secondary evidence? Explain how you have reached this conclusion.

   b) What information do they give about how Robert was killed?

   c) Which of the two sources would be more useful to a historian studying Robert's death? Give reasons for your decision.

3 In pairs:

   a) list the reasons why the Normans took so long to push into Wales

   b) arrange your list in order of importance, giving reasons for your choice

   c) compare your list with the pair sitting next to you. How and why do they differ?

Extension task

4 Study Source 7. Identify examples of biased writing. Suggest reasons for this one-sided reporting.

The story of the prince of Gwynedd: Gruffudd ap Cynan

1

Gruffudd ap Cynan had been forced to spend much of his early life in Dublin, Ireland. This was because of a civil war that went on between the princely families of north Wales.

2

In 1081, Gruffudd landed in north Wales to reclaim his father's kingdom of Gwynedd. This was being ruled by a rival prince, so Gruffudd made a pact with the Norman knight Robert of Rhuddlan, who helped him get his kingdom back.

3

Once Gruffudd had secured his position as the prince of Gwynedd, he turned upon Robert and attacked his castle at Rhuddlan!

4

However, one of Gruffudd's men, Meirion the Red, decided to betray his master to the Normans. Gruffudd was captured and imprisoned in Chester Castle for several years. Gruffudd was eventually rescued by another Welshman, Cynwrig the Tall.

5

In 1088 Gruffudd led a surprise attack on Robert of Rhuddlan's castle at Degannwy, killing Robert on the beach below the castle (see Source 7).

6

However, Hugh the Fat, Earl of Chester, wanted revenge for his cousin's death. Hugh the Fat joined Hugh the Proud, Earl of Shrewsbury, and together they both invaded north Wales. They advanced as far as Anglesey, but Hugh the Proud was killed by an arrow in the eye and the Norman forces retreated.

7

Gruffudd was now recognised as the ruler of lands as far west as the river Clwyd at Rhuddlan. For the next 35 years he ruled this land peacefully and the Normans did not try to advance again.

Source 7

Gruffudd landed with three ships [on the beach below Degannwy castle]. Gruffudd and his men swooped on the lands and carried off men and beasts and hurried back to the boats lying on the beach. Meanwhile the cries of the crowd raised Robert from a mid-day sleep … The fury of this Norman lord, a man as bold as a lion, knew no bounds and he ordered the few men with him to fall on the Welsh. They protested that they were too few in number and that the way down from the top of the rock was too steep. Then Robert, accompanied by only one knight and without his armour, rushed on the enemy. When they saw him with only a shield for protection ... they flung their javelins at this valiant lord, bore down his shield with the weight of their missiles and fatally wounded him. At last the noble warrior, riddled with darts, fell to his knees. Then they rushed up to him, cut off his head and fixed it on the mast of a ship as a sign of victory.

An account of the death of Robert of Rhuddlan in 1088, written by a Norman monk called Orderic Vitalis in the early twelfth century

2.3 Why was there so much conflict in the March of Wales?

In this topic you will find out who the Marcher Lords were, how they settled in Wales and how much power and authority they had over the area they ruled.

Background

The Normans introduced the **manorial system** to England. England was divided into estates, each controlled by a Lord of the Manor. The land belonging to the Manor was worked by peasants, both free and unfree (**serfs**), in return for fixed **dues in kind**, money and services (payment of **taxes**).

The arable land of the Manor was farmed using the three field system. Instead of having all their land in one piece, peasants were given strips of land in each of the three fields. In one strip they might grow wheat, in a strip in another field perhaps barley, and their strip in the third field might be left **fallow** to give the soil a rest. The peasants were allowed to cut the hay on the meadows and graze their cows, sheep and goats on the **common land**. They could gather wood from the waste land and, with the lord's permission, they could bring their pigs into the forest to feed on roots and nuts.

Source 1

▲ An image of the wax seal of Gilbert de Clare, Earl of Gloucester and Marcher Lord of Glamorgan

By 1100 the Normans had been only partially successful in advancing into Wales and for the next two hundred years the border between Wales and England was fought over. This border region became known as the **March of Wales** and the Norman barons who had been granted lordships to protect this region became known as the **Marcher Lords**. The March was not a single unit but a collection of lordships, each ruled over by its own Marcher Lord. The rule of the Marcher Lords lasted from the end of the eleventh century until the Act of Union between England and Wales in 1536. In the regions they conquered, the Marcher Lords introduced the manorial system (see Background).

Powerful Marcher Lords included:

- William Fitzosbern, Earl of Hereford
- Gilbert de Clare, Earl of Gloucester and Marcher Lord of Glamorgan
- William de Braose, Lord of Brycheiniog
- William Marshall, Earl of Pembroke and Chepstow.

ACTIVITY

1 Study Source 1.
   a) What does this source tell you about the power of the Marcher Lords?
   b) What do you think the Lord would have used this seal for?

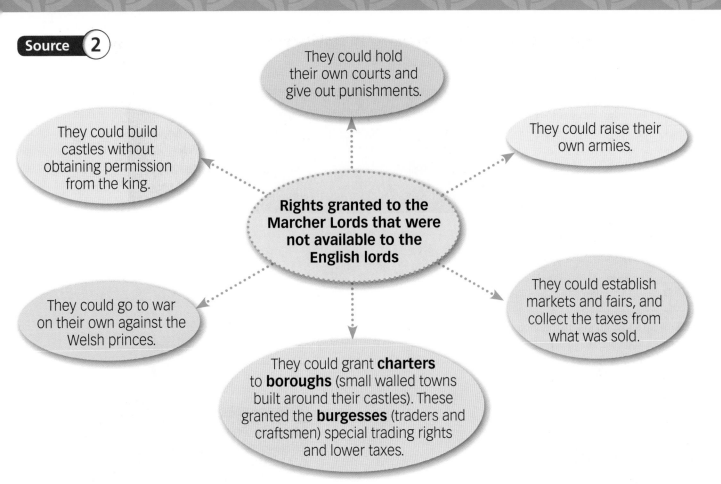

Rights granted to the Marcher Lords that were not available to the English lords

They could hold their own courts and give out punishments.

They could build castles without obtaining permission from the king.

They could raise their own armies.

They could go to war on their own against the Welsh princes.

They could establish markets and fairs, and collect the taxes from what was sold.

They could grant **charters** to **boroughs** (small walled towns built around their castles). These granted the **burgesses** (traders and craftsmen) special trading rights and lower taxes.

Source 2 shows that the Marcher Lords were granted a considerable amount of freedom to rule their lordships. They held different rights and authority to those granted by the king to lords in England. It was said that *'the king's writ did not run in the March of Wales'*, which meant that in practice the king of England often had little control over what these lords did.

ACTIVITY

2 Imagine you are the King of England in 1100. Why might the power of the Marcher Lords prove to be a problem for you? Use Sources 2 and 3 to help you.

 Source 3

For ambitious Normans on the border, Wales was a land of opportunity not under the authority of the English crown. A Norman lord could do in Wales what he could not do in England. He could make war for personal gain in what became a land of almost constant war.

A. D. Carr, *Medieval Wales*, 1995

The settlement of the Marcher lordships followed a familiar pattern:

Source 4

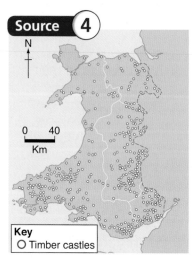

Key
○ Timber castles

▲ Map showing the distribution of motte and bailey castles across the Marcher lordships

Step 1: Conquest and castle building

A Marcher Lord would invade land belonging to a Welsh prince and would either kill him in battle or force him to surrender his land. A castle would then be built to house knights who would patrol this region in the name of the Marcher Lord. Hundreds of motte and bailey castles were built along this border region.

Step 2: The castle becomes the administrative centre of the conquered region

Once a lordship was established the lord's castle would often be rebuilt using stone and would become both the military headquarters and the seat of government for the lord.

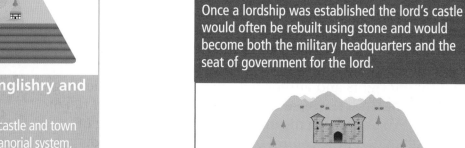

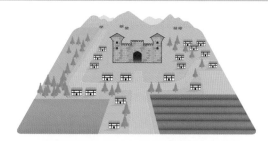

Step 4: Creation of the Englishry and Welshry

On the flat fertile lands around the castle and town the lords introduced the Norman manorial system, with the lord of the manor exercising his rights as landlord over his tenant farmers. This region became known as the **Englishry**. The rest of the lordship, often the more mountainous regions, became known as the **Welshry**. Welsh farmers continued to work the land but now paid their taxes and services to the Marcher Lord rather than to the Welsh prince.

Step 3: Development of a town around the castle

A small town grew up around the castle to serve as a trading centre to supply the needs of the lord and the **garrison** of the castle. The towns of Brecon, Cardiff, Swansea and Haverfordwest all developed in this way.

What type of men were these Marcher Lords?

Violence was common in the March and some Marcher Lords had reputations for being very harsh rulers. One such figure was William de Braose, the Lord of Brycheiniog. In 1175 he carried out the murder of a local Welsh ruler by persuading the ruler to enter his castle at Abergavenny where the man and his family were then killed (see Source 5).

ACTIVITIES

1 Use Sources 4 and 5 to explain *how* the Marcher Lords spread their authority over the areas they conquered.

2 How *much* power and authority did the Marcher Lords exercise over the areas of Wales they ruled?

Source 5

Seisyll ap Dyfnwal (the local Welsh ruler) was slain through treachery in the castle of Abergavenny by the lord of Brycheiniog. And along with him Geoffrey, his son, and the best men of Gwent were slain. And the Normans made for Seisyll's court; and after seizing Gwladus, his wife, they killed Cadwaladr, his son. And on that day there befell a terrible massacre in Gwent. And from that time forth, after the treachery, none of the Welsh dared place trust in the Normans.

From the *Brut y Tywysogyon* [Chronicle of the Princes] written by Welsh monks in the late thirteenth century

Source 6

William Marshall (c.1147–1219)

In 1189 William Marshall, the son of an English knight, married Isabel of Clare, the heiress of Chepstow Castle. A loyal supporter of King Henry II, he was confirmed as Earl of Pembroke and Chepstow in 1198.

To secure his rule over these regions he began a massive castle building programme. He strengthened and enlarged his castles at Chepstow, Usk and Pembroke. Through such a show of strength William was able to exercise firm control over large parts of south Wales. He also granted land for the founding of a Cistercian monastery at Tintern. When he died in 1219, over 70 years old, he was one of the most respected knights in the Welsh Marches.

The tomb effigy of William Marshall, showing him dressed in knightly armour, holding a shield bearing his coat of arms

Done

ACTIVITY

Extension task

3 Use the internet to research the career of one of the Marcher Lords. Write a short biography similar to Source 6 to appear on a website. Mention the castles he built and the area over which he ruled, and try to find some images to add to your biography.

2.4 How did Norman rule change life in Wales?

The Norman occupation resulted in some major changes. On pages 26–29 you will find out about these changes and consider if anything in Wales remained the same

ACTIVITIES

1 Study the information on pages 26–29 and copy and complete the chart below to show how the arrival of the Normans affected Wales. What changed and what stayed the same? You will be able to use this information to help you complete the end of unit assessment.

CHANGE	CONTINUITY
What changed in Wales after the arrival of the Normans?	What stayed the same?

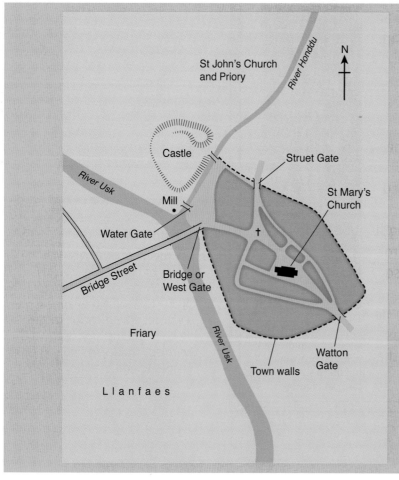

Towns

There were very few towns in Wales before the coming of the Normans. Around the castles there quickly grew small walled towns called boroughs. The traders and craftsmen who lived inside the town walls were English, most of them coming from the lords' estates in England. They were called 'burgesses' and they were granted special privileges to attract them to Wales. These privileges were listed in the town charter. (See page 45.)

◀ Town plan of Brecon showing the castle, the Benedictine priory, the church of St Mary and the town walls which surrounded the borough

▲ The great round keep of Pembroke Castle built by William Marshall around the year 1200

Castles

The first defences built by the Normans were motte and bailey castles. These were often built in haste to secure control of a region. Over time they were replaced with stone castles which had large round towers and high **curtain walls**. These castles were the headquarters of the Norman lord, serving as his office to collect rents and taxes and to administer justice.

The Manor

The Normans introduced manors in the fertile lowlands around the castles and churches. **Bailiffs** were used to make sure the tenant farmers were kept busy tilling, weeding and harvesting. They collected the taxes which included the fee for grinding corn in the lord's mill.

▲ The Lord of the Manor

The Englishry and Welshry

The Welsh lived in the higher, less fertile parts of the lord's land which was known as the Welshry, the flatter area around the manor and town being the Englishry. The old Welsh customs and traditions survived in the Welshry and the tenants lived and farmed much as they had done before, apart from making occasional payments to the lord, mostly in cattle.

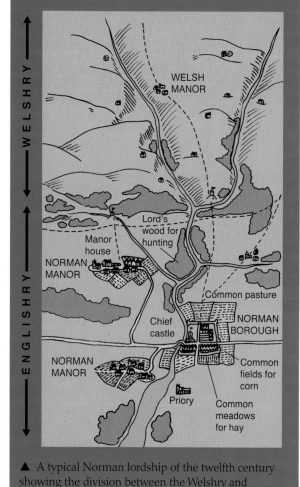

▲ A typical Norman lordship of the twelfth century showing the division between the Welshry and Englishry

The rule of the Welsh kings and princes

In the mountainous parts of Wales, such as Gwynedd, Welsh kings and princes continued to rule as their ancestors had done before them. They raised their own armies and led their men in battle. They acted as law-makers and law-enforcers. They collected taxes. They lived in palaces and encouraged Welsh culture and tradition.

A native Welsh ruler ▶

The Church

Next to their castles the Norman lords built churches constructed of stone instead of wood as were the Welsh churches. They named these churches after saints like Matthew and Peter or the Virgin Mary, instead of the old Celtic saints. Eventually the lords divided Wales into four regions called dioceses, each headed by its own bishop. These first bishops were always Normans.

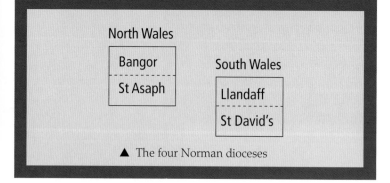

North Wales	South Wales
Bangor	
St Asaph	Llandaff
	St David's

▲ The four Norman dioceses

ACTIVITY

Extension task

2 Norman rule resulted in many changes in Wales. Which do think were the most important changes? Give reasons to support your answer.

Traditional Welsh life

Outside the conquered regions Welsh life remained almost unchanged and the people continued to live in dispersed settlements. The Welsh loved music. They were good singers and played the harp, the crwth (a type of violin) and the pibgorn (a horn-pipe). Bards and poets entertained the people with poetry and story-telling.

The Welsh were proud of their ancestors but they didn't have surnames like we do. Instead, after their first name, they added those of their father and grandfather, for example Gruffudd ap Rhys ap Maredudd.

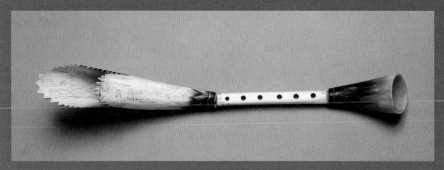

◀ Traditional musical instruments: crwth *(left)*, pibgorn *(below)* ▼

Religious settlements

The Norman lords helped monks to settle in the conquered regions. The first to arrive were the **Benedictines** (Black monks) who built priories like those at Brecon, Monmouth, Carmarthen and Ewenny, close to the Norman castles. They were later followed by the **Cistercians** (White monks) who built monasteries in lonely places like Tintern, Whitland and Valle Crucis. Many Welshmen were later to join the Cistercians.

▼ Tintern Abbey in the late twelfth century

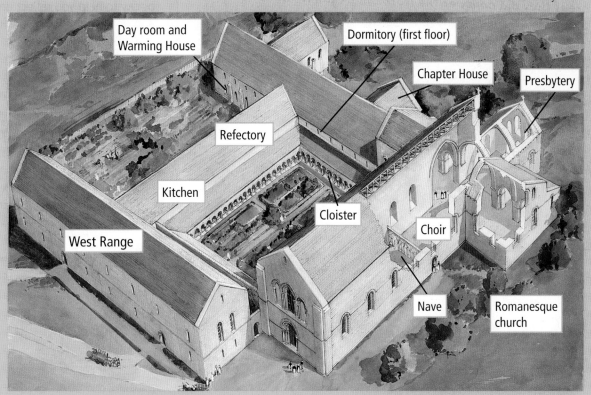

Day room and Warming House

Dormitory (first floor)

Chapter House

Presbytery

Refectory

Kitchen

Cloister

Choir

West Range

Nave

Romanesque church

End of section assessment: Was the coming of the Normans a 'turning point' in Welsh history?

In this section you have found out about how the Normans attempted to conquer Wales. You have studied how the native Welsh rulers attempted to resist the Norman advances. In those areas the Normans did settle, they introduced many changes.

You are now going to write a report which investigates how the arrival of the Normans affected Wales. At the end of the report you will need to make a judgement about whether or not you think these changes resulted in a 'turning point' in Welsh history.

Use the following writing frame to help structure your report.

Question: Was the coming of the Normans a 'turning point' in Welsh history?

During the 1070s the Normans began to push into Wales ... Refer to the creation of the three earldoms and actions of each earl in Wales

These Normans were not successful in conquering all of Wales and they faced fierce opposition from some Welsh rulers ... Give some examples of Welsh resistance

In the areas they did conquer the Normans began to make many changes ... Give some examples of these changes

However, these changes did not affect all of Wales and in those areas the Normans did not conquer traditional Welsh life continued ... Give some examples of how life remained unchanged

In conclusion, I think the coming of the Normans did/did not result in a 'turning point' in Welsh history because ... Give a clear judgement and provide some reasons for your decision

History skills targeted

 Historical knowledge and understanding

 Historical enquiry

 Organisation and communication

REFLECTION AND REVIEW

Now that you have completed your investigation into how Wales was affected by the coming of the Normans you need to reflect upon your learning.

1 How many of the questions you thought up on pages 13 and 19 have you now answered?

2 If you were going to study this unit again think about what you would do differently and the different types of questions you would ask.

3 Copy and complete the triangle below to help you reflect upon and review what you have learnt in studying this unit.

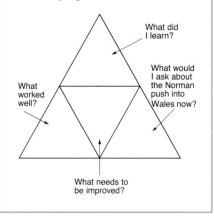

What did I learn?

What would I ask about the Norman push into Wales now?

What worked well?

What needs to be improved?

How successful were the Welsh rulers in resisting English authority between 1135 and 1300?

Section 3

In this section you will learn how to:

⊃ **compare and contrast** the success of native Welsh rulers in resisting the spread of English authority across Wales

⊃ **investigate** the causes and consequences of good and bad relations between the native Welsh rulers and the kings of England

⊃ **make judgements** about the degree of success or failure of individual native Welsh rulers.

In this section you will investigate the attempts by native Welsh rulers to resist the spread of English authority across Wales. In order to complete this investigation you will need to consider the following:

> the success of individual Welsh rulers in spreading their authority over other regions of Wales

> the reaction of the kings of England to the emergence of powerful Welsh rulers

> whether problems facing the king at home in England contributed to the success of the Welsh rulers.

By the end of this investigation you will be able to make a judgement about how successful the native Welsh rulers were in resisting the spread of English authority across Wales between 1135 and 1300.

PLANNING YOUR INVESTIGATION

Before you begin your investigation think about the types of questions you will need to ask to find out how successful the Welsh rulers were in resisting English authority. To help prepare yourself, copy and complete this table.

The attempts by Welsh rulers to resist English authority	
Three things I already know about how the Welsh had resisted English authority (*think about the previous section on the Normans*):	**Three questions** I want to ask to help me in my investigation:

Source ①

In the thirteenth century two princes of Gwynedd – Llywelyn the Great (d.1240) and his grandson Llywelyn the Last (d.1282) – led the Welsh against the English. The two Llywelyns were very powerful rulers.

King Edward I made war against Llywelyn the Last, first of all in 1277 and again in 1282. He defeated and killed the last 'Prince of Wales'. This brought to an end the long struggle between the Welsh and English. The whole of Wales now came to be ruled by the English king and his barons.

A. J. Roderick, *Looking at Welsh History*, 1968

ACTIVITY

What does Source 1 tell you about the attempts by the Welsh princes to resist English authority before 1300?

3.1 Introducing the Welsh rulers

I was born in Gwynedd in 1173.

I took charge of my father's lands in 1195 and became the ruler of Gwynedd by 1200. I then extended my authority across a large part of Wales and became a powerful leader.

I retired to a monastery during the last years of my life and died there in 1240.

I was born in 1223. Llywelyn the Great was my grandfather.

I became the ruler of Gwynedd in 1255 and extended my authority over other parts of Wales.

I led Wales in two wars against English forces under King Edward I. I was killed in an ambush by English knights in December 1282.

Llywelyn ab Iorwerth (Llywelyn the Great)

Llywelyn ap Gruffudd (Llywelyn the Last)

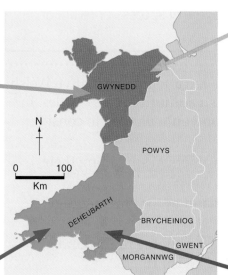

Gwenllian, the Welsh warrior princess

Lord Rhys

I was born in 1097 and was the daughter of Gruffudd ap Cynan, king of Gwynedd.

I married Gruffudd ap Rhys in 1116 and helped him to rule Deheubarth for twenty years. I died in battle in 1136 defending my husband's lands against the Normans.

I was born in 1133 – my mother was Princess Gwenllian.

When my brother Maredudd died in 1155, I became the ruler of Deheubarth. I extended my rule over large parts of south Wales. During the last few years of my life, I was imprisoned by two of my sons who had defeated me in battle. I died in 1197.

Who was king of England at the time?

Key

 – strong king of England   – weak king of England

 King Henry I: 1100–1135
Exercised firm control of his English and French lands

 King Stephen: 1135–1154
The nephew of Henry I. Spent much of his reign fighting a civil war against Matilda, Henry's daughter

 King Henry II: 1154–1189
Spent a large part of his reign on the continent defending his lands in France

 King Richard I (Richard the Lionheart): 1189–1199
Spent most of his reign fighting in the Third Crusade and as a prisoner in France

 King John: 1199–1216
He faced a revolt by his barons and was forced to sign **Magna Carta**

 King Henry III: 1216–1272
He was only nine when he became king and he later faced a rebellion by his barons led by Simon de Montfort

 King Edward I: 1272–1307
He conquered Wales and invaded Scotland

ACTIVITIES

1 Look at the information about the Welsh rulers on page 32 and the kings of England. Match up which kings ruled England at the time of each Welsh ruler.

2 As you read through Section 3, you will learn the stories of the Welsh rulers and how they resisted English authority in Wales. Gather evidence about each ruler so that you can compare and contrast how successful they were in this. Copy and fill in the table below as you go.

Welsh ruler	Evidence of success	Evidence of failure	King of England at the time	King of England's reaction to the Welsh ruler
Gwenllian				
Lord Rhys				
Llywelyn the Great				
Llywelyn the Last				
Rebellions after 1284				

3.2 Why is Gwenllian remembered as 'the Welsh warrior princess'?

In this topic you are going to look at the life of Gwenllian and think about why she has been given the title 'the Welsh warrior princess'. How successful was she in resisting English rule?

Gwenllian's early life and marriage

Gwenllian was born into the princely line of north Wales and was the daughter of Gruffudd ap Cynan, the ruler of Gwynedd. Around 1116, at the age of 18 and against her father's wishes, she ran away to marry Gruffudd ap Rhys, the prince of Deheubarth. The marriage was a happy one and resulted in the birth of four sons.

Gwenllian's training as 'the warrior princess'

The early years of Gruffudd and Gwenllian's marriage were difficult times as King Henry I of England was attempting to impose his authority over south Wales. Gruffudd wanted to push the Normans out of his kingdom of Deheubarth but was having only limited success. In order to avoid capture by the Normans the couple had to live on the run, only emerging from their woodland hideouts to carry out surprise attacks upon Norman settlements. Gwenllian went with her husband on many of these raids and quickly became known as 'the warrior princess' who knew how to handle a sword in battle. She also taught her sons how to use the sword.

What happened when King Henry I died?

In 1135 King Henry I died and for the next two decades England was gripped by civil war as two rivals fought to be the rightful ruler of England. Some supported the claim of Matilda, Henry's daughter; others the claim of Stephen, Henry's nephew. Many Welsh rulers saw this as an opportunity to rise up against Norman rule. Gruffudd ap Rhys realised that if he was to be successful in any rebellion he would need more men and so he decided to visit Gwenllian's father to plead for his support. He took with him his eldest and youngest sons, Maredudd and Rhys, leaving Maelgwn and Morgan behind with Gwenllian.

Gruffudd ap Rhys = Gwenllian

Maredudd	Maelgwn	Morgan	Rhys (Lord Rhys)

▲ Family of Gwenllian

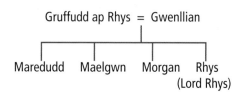

Source ①

Dearest father and mighty king,

To demonstrate the sincerity of our request, my husband makes personal attendance upon your court and I beseech you to consider carefully his intentions.

▲ A letter written by Gwenllian to her father asking for help to fight against the Normans

Gwenllian decides to make a stand

With Gruffudd absent, Maurice de Londres, the Norman lord of Cydweli Castle, decided to attack his lands and force the surrender of the Welsh. When Gwenllian heard of these plans she decided to fight the Normans. She hastily gathered her forces together and marched towards Cydweli Castle. She planned to split her forces: one group would attempt to stop the arrival of Norman reinforcements while the other force would attack the Norman army below Mynydd y Garreg.

The battle of Maes Gwenllian, 1136

Gwenllian had been drawn into a trap set by the Norman lord. Norman reinforcements under the rebel Welshman Gruffudd ap Llywelyn had arrived a day early and had been hidden at the top of Mynydd y Garreg. Gwenllian's forces were now heavily outnumbered and outflanked.

Gwenllian ordered her forces to form a shield wall which held strong until a charge of over 50 Norman knights on horseback broke through. At this point 16-year-old Morgan was fatally wounded and Gwenllian was captured as she cradled her dying child. Her other son Maelgwn was taken prisoner. Before being led away he was forced to watch the execution of his mother. Over 500 Welsh and Norman bodies lay across the battlefield, which has ever since been known as Maes Gwenllian (Gwenllian's field).

Source 2

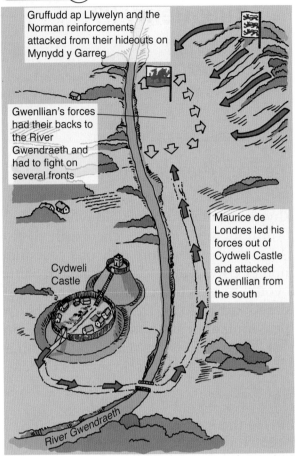

Gruffudd ap Llywelyn and the Norman reinforcements attacked from their hideouts on Mynydd y Garreg

Gwenllian's forces had their backs to the River Gwendraeth and had to fight on several fronts

Maurice de Londres led his forces out of Cydweli Castle and attacked Gwenllian from the south

Cydweli Castle

River Gwendraeth

Source 3

The executioners pulled back Gwenllian's blond plaits and forced her to bend down to reveal the white skin of her neck. The main executioner now looked at Maurice de Londres for the final command to end her life. With the tilt of his head the Norman lord gave the waiting swordsman his consent. Slowly the executioner raised the heavy sword above his head, drew a deep breath and pushed down with considerable force. Just before the razor edge reached its target, a final cry escaped from Gwenllian's lips. 'Remember me!' was her cry – and then there was silence.

From *Gwenllian: The Welsh Warrior Princess* by Peter Newton, 2002

Gruffudd ap Rhys returned too late to help his wife and sons. Within a year Gruffudd himself was dead and his kingdom was ruled by his remaining two sons, Maredudd and Rhys. It was to be many years before the Welsh were able to retake the land lost following the battle of Maes Gwenllian.

ACTIVITIES

1 Use Source 2 and the information on these pages to explain why Gwenllian lost her battle against the Normans in 1136.

2 Fill in your evidence table for Gwenllian (see page 33). How successful was she in resisting English authority?

3 In groups, discuss whether you think Gwenllian deserves the title 'the Welsh warrior princess'. Remember to give reasons for your opinions.

Extension task

4 Source 3 is taken from a biography of Gwenllian in which the author has recreated some of the scenes of her life. What are the problems of using this source to investigate the life of Gwenllian? Why is it useful?

3.3 Was Lord Rhys a threat or a help to King Henry II?

The reign of *Yr Arglwydd Rhys* or Lord Rhys, who ruled from 1155 to 1197, provides a good example of how one Welsh region, Deheubarth, emerged as a powerful Welsh kingdom with a strong Welsh ruler, despite the actions of a forceful English king, Henry II. But was Lord Rhys more of a threat or a help to English rule?

Source **1**

The Lord Rhys was the greatest of the princes of Deheubarth, and one of the outstanding leaders of Welsh independence.

W. P. Wheldon, *Famous Welshmen*, 1944

The rise to power of Rhys ap Gruffudd (Lord Rhys)

Rhys was only four years old when his father, Gruffudd, the Prince of Deheubarth, died in 1137, which was in turn only one year after his mother Gwenllian had been killed in battle. As a youth he watched his older brother Maredudd build up Deheubarth, pushing out the Norman barons from large parts of south-east Wales. Following Maredudd's death in 1155 Rhys became the sole ruler of Deheubarth.

The effects of the new king

In 1154 there was a new king of England. Henry II was keen to assert his authority and in 1158 Rhys was forced to submit to Henry and acknowledge his **overlordship**. Rhys had to give up much of Deheubarth, keeping only the central region around his castle at Dinefwr. As he had been forced to accept the power of the new king of England, it seemed that he had little hope of getting back his lands. He was also forced to adopt the title of Lord in place of King.

Challenging the power of King Henry II

In 1164 Rhys joined with Owain Gwynedd of north Wales in a major revolt against Henry's rule. By 1165 Rhys had won back the lands that had been taken away from him in 1158. Alarmed at the growth of Welsh resistance, Henry led an invasion force into Wales from Oswestry in the summer of 1165. However, heavy rain and bad weather forced him to retreat without doing battle. Problems with Archbishop Beckett stopped him from returning to Wales.

Henry II's change of policy towards Lord Rhys

In 1169 a Norman army invaded Ireland in support of Dermot, King of Leinster, who was facing a rebellion against his rule. Dermot had won the support of the Marcher Lords, especially Richard de Clare, Earl of Pembroke. Henry was concerned that success in Ireland would increase the power of the Marcher Lords and in 1171 he decided to travel to Ireland to sort out the problem. As he travelled through south Wales to Ireland he met with Lord Rhys and the two men came to an agreement.

Source **2**

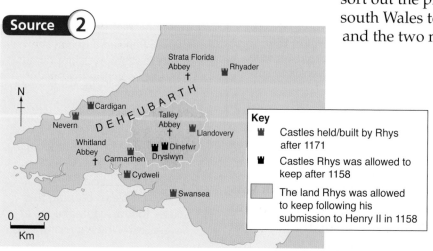

Strata Florida Abbey

Rhyader

N

Cardigan

Talley Abbey

Nevern

D E H E U B A R T H

Llandovery

Whitland Abbey

Dinefwr

Carmarthen Dryslwyn

Cydweli

Swansea

0   20
Km

Key

⬛ Castles held/built by Rhys after 1171

⬛ Castles Rhys was allowed to keep after 1158

The land Rhys was allowed to keep following his submission to Henry II in 1158

◀ Map showing the reduced land area left to Lord Rhys after 1158

Becoming King Henry's Justiciar of South Wales

By the agreement of 1171 Henry recognised Rhys as ruler of Deheubarth and officially returned to him all the land taken away in 1158. He also appointed him **Justiciar** of south Wales. Henry had come to see Rhys as a useful ally who was sufficiently powerful to check the growing strength of the Marcher Lords. Lord Rhys was now not only the ruler of his own lands but also the King of England's representative, the man Henry relied on to keep an eye on the power of the Marcher Lords. Until Henry's death in 1189 there was peace between the two former enemies.

Building castles to protect his borders

Henry allowed Lord Rhys to protect his borders by building castles. Rhys already had stone castles at Dryslwyn and Dinefwr and to these he now added castles at Cardigan, Rhyader, Llandovery and Nevern to guard his borders. Lord Rhys chose the castle at Cardigan as the centre of his administration.

Becoming a champion of Welsh tradition and culture

In 1176 a festival of poetry and music was held at Cardigan. It was Wales' first **Eisteddfod**. Poets and musicians came from all parts of Wales to take part in the competitions. Rhys was a generous patron to the Cistercian abbeys at Whitland and Strata Florida, and he also founded an abbey at Talley. After he died the poets praised him as one of the champions of Welsh independence.

The last years of Lord Rhys

The death of Henry II in 1189 ended the long years of peace as the new king, Richard I (the Lionheart), was less interested in winning the friendship of Lord Rhys. As relations grew tense, Lord Rhys decided to strike first and he attacked several Norman castles across south Wales. During Richard's absence on crusade, Lord Rhys was successful in expanding his lands.

However, during this war, trouble erupted between the sons of Lord Rhys over their inheritance. In 1194 two of them turned on their father and imprisoned him for a while. When Lord Rhys died in 1197 a power struggle developed between the sons and Deheubarth was divided up between them. The unity built up by Lord Rhys was now lost.

▲ The tomb effigy of Lord Rhys in St David's Cathedral, Pembrokeshire

Source 3

ACTIVITIES

1 The *Brut y Tywysogyon* (Chronicle of the Princes) is an important primary source for Welsh history. It is a record of information about the rulers of the kingdoms of Wales and was written by Welsh monks. Write an entry about Lord Rhys for each of the following years: 1155, 1158, 1171, 1189, 1194, 1197.

   Make sure you include information on:
   - the military successes and failures of Lord Rhys
   - his relationship with Henry II and Richard I
   - his relationship with his sons
   - the castles he built.

2 In pairs, create two lists to sort out the information and evidence on these pages. Use the following headings:
   a) Lord Rhys was seen as a threat by Henry II
   b) Lord Rhys proved himself useful to Henry II

   Look at your completed lists and weigh up the evidence. Overall do you think Lord Rhys was more of a threat or a help to King Henry II?

3 Fill in your evidence table for Lord Rhys (see page 33). How successful was he in resisting English authority?

Extension task

4 Read Source 1 on page 36. What information can you find from pages 36–37 to support the comments made in the source?

3.4 Does Llywelyn ab Iorwerth deserve the title 'Llywelyn the Great'?

Llywelyn ab Iorwerth started life as a prince of Gwynedd in north Wales. This topic will show you how he won the support of King John and extended his authority throughout larger parts of Wales to emerge as a powerful leader. He became known as Llywelyn the Great and you will find out why he got this title and think about whether he deserved it.

Llywelyn was born into the princely house of Gwynedd but, as his father had died when he was an infant, his father's lands were divided between his uncles and cousins. In 1195, Llywelyn decided to take control of his father's lands and then to expand his rule over the neighbouring Welsh kingdoms. To do this he faced some challenges.

▲ Carved stone head thought to be a likeness of Llywelyn ab Iorwerth

His family
Llywelyn was in competition with his uncles and cousins to become the ruler of Gwynedd.

Welsh rulers
To extend his authority outside Gwynedd, Llywelyn would need to impose his overlordship over the other Welsh princes.

What challenges did Llywelyn face in expanding his rule over the kingdoms of Wales?

The King of England
King John, who was King of England at the time, would not want to see the emergence of a powerful ruler of Gwynedd and would take action to stop such a development.

Marcher Lords
The Marcher Lords (see pages 22–25) would take action to protect their land along the Welsh border and would also be looking to expand their influence in Wales.

ACTIVITIES

1 Copy the headings in the spider diagram above. Using the information on page 39 about Llywelyn's rise to power, add to the infomation on each of the four challenges and give examples of how he overcame them.

2 Study the information on pages 38–39. In pairs, debate the argument that Llywelyn deserves the title 'Llywelyn the Great'. One person should argue for and one person should argue against. Then decide between yourselves which argument is more persuasive.

3 Fill in your evidence table for Llywelyn the Great (see page 33). How successful was he in resisting English authority?

> **Source** 1
>
> In that year (1233) Llywelyn, and a mighty host along with him, went to Brycheiniog, and he burned all the towns and castles that were in that land, and he carried away many spoils with him. And he laid siege to the castle of Brecon every day for a whole month with catapults, and he threw (destroyed) the walls to the ground.
>
> From the *Brut y Tywysogyon* (Chronicle of the Princes) written by Welsh monks in the late thirteenth century

Llywelyn's rise to power

Llywelyn used military force to fight against his uncles and cousins and by 1201 he was the sole ruler of Gwynedd. →

Llywelyn now had to secure the friendship and support of King John of England. To do this he married the king's illegitimate daughter Joan in 1205. →

By 1210, through a combination of military force in battles and creating friendship alliances with rivals, Llywelyn had extended his authority over neighbouring Welsh rulers and he was recognised as their overlord. →

The growth of Llywelyn's power worried the English king and during 1210–11 King John invaded Wales twice, forcing Llywelyn to surrender. Joan negotiated with her father and he allowed Llywelyn to remain ruler of Gwynedd, although he lost his other territories. ↓

To protect his realm Llywelyn copied the English king and the Marcher Lords and built castles. They included Dolwyddelan, Castell y Bere, Dolbadarn, Degannwy and Criccieth. Built of stone, many had a distinctive 'D'-shaped tower, a heavily defended entrance with ditches and gate-towers. They served as a badge of power and status. ←

To protect his border with the land of the Marcher Lords, Llywelyn arranged for four of his daughters to be married into the powerful families of the March of Wales. His son, Dafydd, was married to Isabella, the daughter of William de Braose, the Lord of Brecon, Builth and Abergavenny. ←

King John died in 1216 and was succeeded by his son Henry III, aged nine. This provided Llywelyn with the opportunity to regain his lost territories and by 1218 he had reclaimed control over native Wales. ←

King John faced his own problems. When John's barons rose against him in 1214, Llywelyn joined with the barons. The king was forced to sign Magna Carta in 1215 and he allowed Llywelyn to adopt the title 'Prince of Aberffraw and Lord of Snowdon'.

Llywelyn as patron of Welsh culture and tradition

Llywelyn ensured that Welshmen were chosen as bishops of St David's and Bangor. He was a generous patron to the Cistercian monks and their abbeys at Strata Florida, Aberconwy and Cymer. He founded a Franciscan priory at Llanfaes on Anglesey. He was also generous in his support of the bards.

The last years of Llywelyn the Great

In 1238 Llywelyn called all the rulers of Wales together at Strata Florida Abbey to get them to recognise his son Dafydd as his successor. Llywelyn did not want to divide his lands and when his other son Gruffudd protested he had him put in prison.

During the last years of his life Llywelyn retired to the monastery of Aberconwy. He died there in 1240.

REVIEWING YOUR INVESTIGATION

a) How many of the questions that you asked at the start of this investigation (see page 31) have been answered so far?

b) Think of some other questions that you would now like to ask to further your investigation.

Source 2

Degannwy
Dolbadarn
GWYNEDD Dolwyddelan
Criccieth

Castell y Bere

N

0   30
Km

Key
- Castles built by Llywelyn ab Iorwerth
- Expansion of Gwynedd by Llewelyn ab Iorwerth

▲ Map showing the extent of the land ruled by Llywelyn ab Iorwerth in 1234

Source 3

Having started with nothing, Llywelyn ended his days as Prince of Wales in all but name, having achieved this position entirely through his political and military ability.

A. D. Carr, a professor of Welsh History, writing in his book *Medieval Wales*, 1995

3.5 Why was Llywelyn ap Gruffudd, Prince of Wales, successful against Henry III but unsuccessful against Edward I?

Llywelyn ap Gruffudd became ruler of Gwynedd in 1255, but wanted to extend his rule over other kingdoms in Wales. To do this he had to resist English authority first from Henry III and then from Edward I. In this topic you will look at how successful he was against each king.

The changing kingdom of Gwynedd between 1240 and 1255

After the death of Llywelyn the Great in 1240, Wales was ruled by his son Dafydd ap Llywelyn. Despite the promises of loyalty made to Llywelyn the Great at Strata Florida Abbey in 1238 (see page 39), several Welsh rulers gave support to Dafydd's half-brother, Gruffudd. King Henry III of England had Gruffudd taken prisoner but in 1244 Gruffudd fell to his death while trying to escape from the Tower of London (see Source 1).

Dafydd died in 1246, leaving no sons. Now three of Gruffudd's sons began a long-drawn-out fight to become the ruler of Gwynedd. In 1247 Henry III invaded Gwynedd and in the peace settlement he took away much of their land. Fighting continued among Gruffudd's sons until 1255 when Llywelyn finally defeated his brothers Owain and Dafydd at the battle of Bryn Derwin. As a result of this victory he was now sole ruler of Gwynedd and he could set his sights on expanding his lands outside north-west Wales.

Source 1

▲ Gruffudd ap Llywelyn falling to his death from the Tower of London in 1244. The knotted bedclothes and curtains he had used to make a rope snapped

Source 2

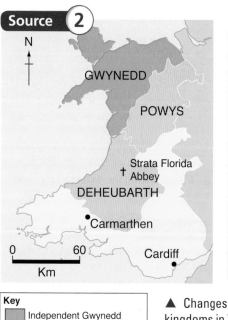

Key
- Independent Gwynedd
- Subject to Gwynedd
- Lands of the Marcher Lords

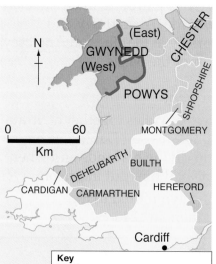

▲ Changes to the kingdoms in Wales between 1240 (left) and 1247 (right)

Key
- Independent Gwynedd
- Independent of Gwynedd
- Subject to the King of England
- Limit to the state of Gwynedd
- Lands of the Marcher Lords

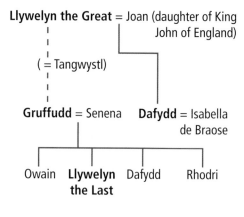

▲ Family tree: Llywelyn the Last

ACTIVITY

1 Write and illustrate four boxes to create a storyboard of the kingdom of Gwynedd and its rulers between 1240 and 1255.

ACTIVITY

2 How successful was Llywelyn ap Gruffudd against King Henry III? To find out, start by copying the table below. Now read about each event described on this page.

For each event, write a summary version in the column of the person who benefited more. Then decide how important this event was to him, by awarding a score of 1, 2 or 3 (3 = most important).

Round One			
Llywelyn ap Gruffudd		**King Henry III**	
Event	Score	Event	Score

Source ③

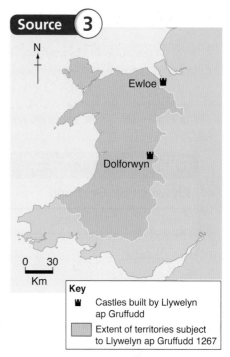

▲ Map showing the extent of Llywelyn's authority in Wales in 1267

Key
🏰 Castles built by Llywelyn ap Gruffudd
▢ Extent of territories subject to Llywelyn ap Gruffudd 1267

ROUND ONE: THE RISE OF THE 'PRINCE OF WALES'

LLYWELYN AP GRUFFUDD

KING HENRY III

– VS –

1 After 1255 Llywelyn set about extending his authority over other parts of Wales. By 1257 he ruled the north Wales coast as far as Chester, and had pushed into Powys in the east and Deheubarth in the south.

2 In 1258 Llywelyn adopted the title 'Prince of Wales', forcing the other Welsh rulers to swear loyalty to him rather than to Henry III.

3 In 1264 Henry III faced a rebellion by his barons who were led by Simon de Montfort. Llywelyn sided with de Montfort and agreed to marry his daughter, Eleanor. De Montfort was killed in battle in 1265.

4 Problems with his barons meant that Henry III had to make peace with Llywelyn. By the Treaty of Montgomery signed in 1267 Henry recognised Llywelyn as Prince of Wales and restored to him all the land he had taken away in 1247.

5 The other Welsh rulers now recognised Llywelyn as their overlord and allowed him to speak on their behalf with the king. Llywelyn was the first ruler to use the title 'Prince of Wales'.

ACTIVITIES

3 Look at your completed table from Activity 2. Who benefited more overall? Think about each event and how much impact it had on the rulers. In your opinion which ruler won Round One, Llywelyn ap Gruffudd or King Henry III? Remember to give reasons to support your decision.

4 Give three reasons why Llywelyn ap Gruffudd was able to use the title 'Prince of Wales' by 1267.

5 Fill in your evidence table for Llywelyn the Last (see page 33). How successful was he in resisting English authority at this stage of his reign?

ACTIVITY

1 How successful was Llywelyn ap Gruffudd against King Edward I?

To investigate, copy the table below and read about the events described in the boxes on pages 42–43. For each event, write a summary version in the column of the person who benefited more. Then decide how important this event was to him, by awarding a score of 1, 2 or 3 (3 = most important).

Round Two			
Llywelyn ap Gruffudd		**King Edward I**	
Event	Score	Event	Score

Background

Edward I was a very different man to his father Henry III. He had a more powerful personality and was determined to make himself master of the whole of Britain. He intended to impose his authority over Wales and Scotland. He invaded Wales on two occasions and during his Scottish campaign he was given the nickname 'the Hammer of the Scots'.

ROUND TWO: THE CLASH OF THE TITANS

LLYWELYN AP GRUFFUDD

KING EDWARD I

– VS –

Source 4

▲ King Edward I

1 In 1272 Henry III died. Llywelyn refused to attend the **coronation** of Edward I, claiming he could not trust his safety to the new king.

2 Relations between Llywelyn and Edward quickly grew worse. Llywelyn refused to renew his **homage** to Edward on five occasions between 1274 and 1276, even when Edward took his entire court to Chester in 1275.

3 Edward was furious and decided to force Llywelyn to obey him. He captured Eleanor, Simon de Montfort's daughter, who was sailing from France to Wales to marry Llywelyn and refused to release her. Even this did not make Llywelyn give in.

4 Edward now won the support of the Marcher Lords who were concerned over the growth of Llywelyn's power. He also won the support of Llywelyn's brother, Dafydd. In November 1276 Edward took the decision to invade Wales to deal with 'the rebel and disturber of the peace'.

5 Edward sent three armies into Wales. They cut a path towards Gwynedd from Chester, Montgomery and Carmarthen. Edward's fleet captured Anglesey which meant his men were then able to cut off the food supplies to Gwynedd. Llywelyn was forced to submit.

6 By the Treaty of Aberconwy in 1277, Llywelyn lost all his lands except for Gwynedd. He had to pay homage to the king in London. Edward ordered castles to be built at Flint, Rhuddlan, Aberystwyth and Builth to surround Gwynedd.

7 In 1278 Edward allowed Llywelyn to marry Eleanor in Worcester Cathedral.

8 On Palm Sunday 1282, Dafydd, who had been given lands east of the river Conwy as a reward for helping Edward, rose up in rebellion against the English forces. Llywelyn had little choice but to join the rebellion.

9 Edward was now forced to invade Wales for a second time. His armies attacked Gwynedd from three different directions. Not wanting to be encircled in Snowdonia, Llywelyn led his army south towards Builth Wells in mid-Wales.

10 At Cilmeri on 11 December 1282, Llywelyn, who was away from the main body of his army on a scouting mission, was spotted by a group of English knights. They attacked and during the fight Llywelyn was killed. He was speared through the chest by Stephen de Frankton.

ACTIVITIES

2 Look at your completed table from Activity 1. Who benefited more overall? Think about each event and how much impact it had on the rulers. In your opinion which ruler won Round Two, Llywelyn ap Gruffudd or King Edward I? Remember to give reasons to support your decision.

3 Give three reasons why relations between Llywelyn ap Gruffudd and Edward I broke down between 1272 and 1277.

4 Would you have advised Llywelyn ap Gruffudd to join in the rebellion against English rule started by his brother Dafydd on Palm Sunday 1282? Support your advice with reasons.

5 Write an account of the last year of Llywelyn ap Gruffudd's reign as it might have appeared in the *Brut y Tywysogyon* (Chronicle of the Princes). Remember that this was written by Welsh monks.

6 Fill in the rest of your evidence table for Llywelyn the Last (see page 33). How successful was he in resisting English authority at this stage of his reign?

7 Explain why Llywelyn ap Gruffudd was successful in resisting the authority of Henry III but unsuccessful in resisting the authority of Edward I. When writing your answer you should think about:

- the dispute between Henry III and his barons
- Llywelyn's friendship with the rebellious English barons
- the differences between Henry III and Edward I as rulers
- Llywelyn's refusal to show respect to royal authority
- the attitude of the Marcher Lords towards Llywelyn
- the behaviour of Dafydd, Llywelyn's brother.

3.6 Did Wales lose its independence with the death of Llywelyn the Last?

When Llywelyn the Last was killed in 1282, King Edward I divided the kingdom of Gwynedd into shires which were ruled by English officials. He encircled north Wales with castles and encouraged English merchants to settle in the new towns built alongside the castles. Was this the end of Welsh independence?

The collapse of the house of Gwynedd

The *Brut y Tywysogyon* (Chronicle of the Princes) ends its account of the year 1282 with the words, 'then all Wales was cast to the ground'. After Llywelyn's death at Cilmeri (see page 43) his head was cut off and it was sent to London and placed on a spear on one of the gates to the Tower of London (see Source 1).

Llywelyn's wife, Eleanor, had died in childbirth in June 1282 and now his heir, a daughter named Gwenllian, was sent to England. She was made to spend her life as a nun at Sempringham in Lincolnshire, never hearing a word of Welsh spoken. Llywelyn's brother, Dafydd, was captured by Edward's forces and was executed in Shrewsbury. His head was sent to join that of his brother at the Tower. The house of Gwynedd was now shell-shocked and without a strong leader.

The Edwardian settlement of Wales

The creation of shires and the appointment of royal officials

In March 1284 Edward issued his *Statute of Rhuddlan*. This laid down how he intended to rule the **Principality**.

Source 1

▲ Llywelyn's head is paraded through the streets of London on its way to the Tower

Source 2

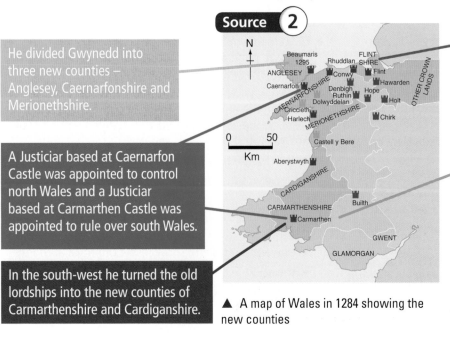

He divided Gwynedd into three new counties – Anglesey, Caernarfonshire and Merionethshire.

He created the new county of Flintshire in the north-east which was to come under the control of the earldom of Chester.

A Justiciar based at Caernarfon Castle was appointed to control north Wales and a Justiciar based at Carmarthen Castle was appointed to rule over south Wales.

He left the borderlands in the hands of the Marcher Lords.

In the south-west he turned the old lordships into the new counties of Carmarthenshire and Cardiganshire.

▲ A map of Wales in 1284 showing the new counties

Key
- ♜ Royal castles
- ♜ Castles built by the Marcher Lords
- ♜ Former Welsh castles now under Edward's control
- the Principality (showing the new shires)
- the Marcher Lords

Map labels: Beaumaris 1295, ANGLESEY, Caernarfon, CAERNARFONSHIRE, Criccieth, Harlech, MERIONETHSHIRE, Dolwyddelan, Rhuddlan, FLINT SHIRE, Conwy, Flint, Hawarden, Denbigh, Hope, Ruthin, Holt, Chirk, OTHER CROWN LANDS, Castell y Bere, Aberystwyth, CARDIGANSHIRE, Builth, CARMARTHENSHIRE, Carmarthen, GWENT, GLAMORGAN

The new shires were to last for over 700 years. English officials were appointed to rule each shire. The highest official was the **sheriff**, and below him was the **chamberlain** who supervised the finances. A new system of courts was set up, operating English law not Welsh law. English was the language used for official purposes. The Welsh population bitterly resented this layer of English authority imposed upon their lives. They also resented the new castles which were seen as the hated badges of English royal authority.

The building of a ring of castles

To impose his authority over the defeated regions of Wales, Edward ordered the building of a chain of castles, designed to surround Gwynedd (see Source 2).

After his invasion of 1277 he had built castles at Flint and Rhuddlan. Following the events of 1282–83 he now ordered new castles at Caernarfon, Conwy and Harlech and, after 1294–95, at Beaumaris. All of them were situated on the coast so that they could be supplied by sea and avoid a siege. The existing Welsh castles at Criccieth and Castell y Bere were strengthened and enlarged.

The building of castles was a massive and costly undertaking. Supplies of stone, timber and other raw materials had to be carefully organised under the management of Edward's architect, Master James of St George. Men had to be brought from all the English counties to help with the building work.

> **Source 3**
>
> The castles built by King Edward were feared and hated by the Welsh people of his time. They represented conquest and the failure of the Welsh people in their struggle for independence.
>
> Catrin Stevens, historian, writing in her book *Wales in the Middle Ages*, 1992

Source 4

The Welsh had very restricted access into the walled town

English merchants were protected by heavily defended town walls

The defended harbour made it difficult to lay siege to the castle

The castle was situated on a rocky outcrop surrounded by water on two sides

▲ An artist's impression of the castle and borough town of Conwy around the year 1300

The creation of borough towns

Edward ordered the building of towns or boroughs next to the castles. To protect them they were surrounded by a heavily defended curtain wall, with regular watch towers and defended entrances. The towns were intended to be trading centres but only English merchants were allowed to set up within the borough. Charters granted the traders or burgesses special trading privileges (see page 27). This particularly annoyed the Welsh merchants who were not allowed such privileges. During the rebellions of the 1290s the towns became the main targets of attack by the Welsh rebels.

▼ The charter granted to the burgesses of Denbigh town in October 1285 by the Marcher Lord, Henry de Lacy. It granted 63 named burgesses special trading rights within the town. In return, each burgess was obliged to pay a small rent and provide one armed man 'for the guard and defence' of the town

Source 5

Rebellions after 1284

In the years immediately after the Edwardian conquest there were several rebellions by the native Welsh. In 1287 the revolt by Rhys ap Maredudd in south Wales was easily and quickly put down, but the revolt of Madog ap Llywelyn in north Wales between 1294–95 was more serious, lasting for nine months.

The rebellion of Madog ap Llywelyn, 1294–95

English rule was unpopular. Many Welsh people resented having to pay higher taxes and to provide men for service in the king's army in France; and the harsh rule of the officials in the shires who collected rents and imposed fines was particularly disliked. In the summer of 1294 Madog ap Llywelyn, a cousin of the last Welsh prince, rose up in rebellion. The opening move was the defeat of the Earl of Lincoln near Denbigh, followed by the attack and capture of the town and castle of Caernarfon in September. Many of Caernarfon's buildings were set on fire (see Source 7). The sheriff of Anglesey, Roger de Pulesdon, was captured and hanged. The rising showed how much resentment against English rule had built up in the few years since the conquest of 1284.

Source 6

A charter gives the burgesses very special rights and privileges. They can carry weapons to protect themselves against us, the Welsh. One of them acts as a watchman at night, and rings a bell every two hours to say that all is well. On top of that, Edward has given every burgess a piece of land called a burgage. The burgess doesn't have to pay rent on this for ten years. Another annoying thing is that we, the Welsh, can only buy and sell our goods outside the new borough town walls. We even have to pay tolls for this favour. This makes us feel like outsiders in our own country. It's so unfair.

An interview with a Welsh merchant living in the 1290s, as imagined by the historian Catrin Stevens. The merchant describes his attitude towards the new borough towns created by Edward I

▶ An artist's impression of the attack by the forces of Madog ap Llywelyn upon Caernarfon Castle and town in September 1294. The Welsh forces broke through the town walls and set fire to the buildings inside and to parts of the castle itself

Edward led an invasion force into Wales but during Christmas 1294 he was besieged inside Conwy Castle until relief forces arrived by sea. Eventually the mightier English forces overcame the rebels. Madog was captured and he spent the rest of his life imprisoned in the Tower of London. The seat of Madog's power at Llanfaes on Anglesey was destroyed and in its place Edward ordered the building of a new castle – Beaumaris.

In 1301 Edward made his eldest son, Edward of Caernarfon, 'Prince of Wales' and since that time the male heir to the English crown has been given that title. Was this the final sign that Wales had lost its independence?

ACTIVITIES

1 Make up a group of three pairs. Each pair should look at one of the changes introduced in Wales by Edward I after 1284: the creation of shires and the appointment of royal officials; the building of castles; and the creation of borough towns. They should present a short role play to the rest of their group, where they act as a couple of Welsh people discussing what they didn't like about the changes made.

2 What reasons are given in Source 6 to explain why many Welsh people disliked the new borough towns?

3 Study Source 7. Write two paragraphs describing the rebellion of Madog ap Llywelyn in 1294–95. The paragraphs will describe the same event but paragraph one should be written from the viewpoint of a supporter of Madog, and paragraph two from the viewpoint of a supporter of Edward I.

4 Fill in your evidence table for 'Rebellions after 1284' (see page 33). How successful were the rebellions in resisting English authority?

5 Did the death of Llywelyn ap Gruffudd in 1282 see the end of Welsh independence? In writing your answer, think about:
   • the creation of shires
   • the building of castles
   • the employment of English officials
   • the creation of borough towns
   • privileges granted to English merchants
   • the collection of rents and taxes by English officials.

End of section assessment: How successful were the Welsh rulers in resisting English authority between 1135 and 1300?

In this section you have found out about how the native Welsh rulers tried to resist the attempts of the kings of England to spread their authority over all parts of Wales. On some occasions individual Welsh princes were successful in extending their authority, while at other times a strong English king caused an extension of English rule across Wales.

You are now going to look at your completed evidence table (see page 33 at the start of this section) to investigate the success of the various Welsh rulers in resisting English authority between 1135 and 1300.

Welsh ruler	Evidence of success	Evidence of failure	King of England at the time	King of England's reaction to the Welsh ruler
Gwenllian				
Lord Rhys				
Llywelyn the Great				
Llywelyn the Last				
Rebellions after 1284				

1 Study the information you have written in the 'Evidence of success' column. Rank the successes in order of importance, the most successful first and the least successful last. Give reasons for each choice.

2 Compare your list with the person sitting next to you. Do the rank orders differ? If so, how, and why?

3 Study the information you have written in the last column: 'King of England's reaction to the Welsh ruler'. What reasons can you give to explain why some kings of England were successful in their dealings with Welsh rulers but others were not so successful? Remember to explain your reasons.

4 Using the information you have gathered in your answers to questions 1 and 3, your own knowledge of this period and internet research, create a PowerPoint presentation with the title, 'How successful were the Welsh rulers in resisting English authority between 1135 and 1300?' You should create a slide for each Welsh ruler, working from the least successful to the most successful, and give details about evidence of success and evidence of failure.

REFLECTION AND REVIEW:

Now that you have completed your investigation into how Welsh rulers attempted to resist the spread of English authority over Wales between 1135 and 1300 you need to reflect upon your learning.

1 How many of the questions you thought up on pages 31 and 39 have you now answered?

2 If you were going to study this unit again think about what you would do differently and the different types of questions you would ask.

3 Copy and complete the triangle below to help you reflect upon and review what you have learnt in studying this unit.

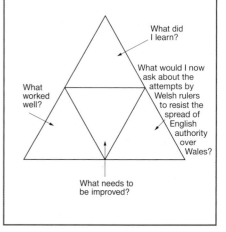

How far did life in Wales change between 1300 and 1500?

In this section you will learn how to:

⊃ **examine** how Wales changed between 1300 and the end of the medieval period in 1500

⊃ **understand** how events in these two centuries brought about change

⊃ **make judgements** about how these changes affected life in Wales.

In this section you will investigate some of the key events that helped to shape life in Wales over the course of two centuries, between the years 1300 and 1500. In order to complete this investigation you will need to consider the following:

> the main features of Welsh life, culture and tradition in 1300 compared with 1500

> the impact of the Black Death upon Wales

> the main religious changes to affect Wales

> the reasons why the Welsh rebelled against English rule at the start of the fourteenth century but supported royal authority at the end of that century.

By the end of the investigation you will be able to make a judgement about how far life in Wales had changed by the end of the medieval period in 1500.

PLANNING YOUR INVESTIGATION

Before you begin your investigation think about the types of questions you will need to ask to find out how far life in Wales had changed by the end of the medieval period. To help prepare yourself, copy and fill in this table.

How far did life in Wales change between 1300 and 1500?	
Three things I already know about what Wales was like in 1300 (*think about how it was ruled and the lives of Welsh people*):	**Three questions** I want to ask to help me in my investigation:

Source 1

For two centuries, from 1282 to 1485, the Welsh were governed as a conquered people. During that time great social changes were taking place. The old Welsh tribal groupings in the uplands of Wales were tending to disintegrate, and so were the manors which had been formed in the lowlands by the Norman lords. In the middle of the fourteenth century the Black Death speeded up these changes. The social distress caused by the plague and the breaking of the old order added to the misery and hardship of the people which helped cause the revolt of Owain Glyndŵr in 1400.

David Williams, *A Short History of Modern Wales,* 1951

ACTIVITY

What does Source 1 tell you about changes to life in Wales between 1282 and 1485?

4.1 What was Wales like in 1300?

By 1300 Wales was beginning to adjust to the changes introduced by King Edward I following his victory over the independent Welsh princes in the war of 1282–83 (see pages 42–43). Edward had imposed changes on how Wales was governed and these changes were now beginning to result in economic and social changes. On pages 50–53 you will investigate what Wales was like in 1300.

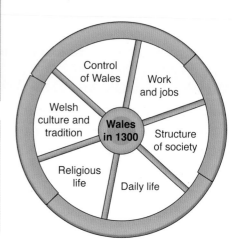

ACTIVITY

Your task is to create a snapshot of what life was like in Wales in 1300.

a) Draw a larger version of the wheel diagram on the right.

b) Now use the information on pages 50–53 to list four bullet points in each segment to describe the key features under that heading.

Source **1**

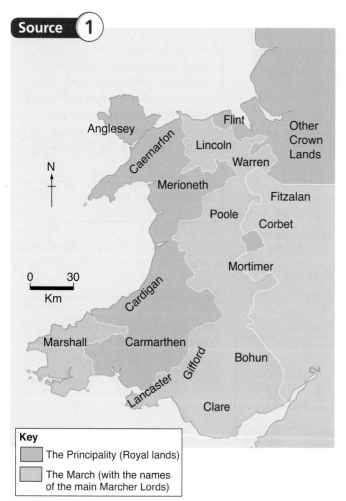

Key

◻ The Principality (Royal lands)

◻ The March (with the names of the main Marcher Lords)

How was Wales governed in 1300?

By 1300 all of Wales was under English authority. The country was split into two parts: the Principality and the March.

The Principality was made up of the old kingdoms of Gwynedd, Powys and Deheubarth, and was now under the direct control of the king. The March remained in the hands of the Marcher Lords who had ruled there since the Norman Conquest.

Within the Principality English law replaced Welsh law and the highest posts in local government were filled by Englishmen. Some of these officials exercised their authority in a harsh way, especially when it came to the collection of taxes. Over time this resulted in increased political tension across Wales.

◀ Map of Wales in 1300 showing the Principality and the Marcher Lordships (together with names of the main Marcher Lords)

How was religion organised in Wales?

The Normans had divided Wales into four dioceses (St David's, Llandaff, Bangor and St Asaph), each headed by its own bishop, and each diocese was sub-divided into parishes. Each parish had its own church and priest. People were very religious and they believed that in order to get to heaven they had to attend church regularly on a Sunday. While the priests would be Welshmen, the bishops were nearly always Englishmen. This became a major cause of concern after 1300 (see page 57).

The Normans also helped to spread monasteries across Wales, first through the Benedictines and later the Cistercian monks. These monasteries became increasingly important in both the religious and economic life of Wales during the thirteenth and fourteenth centuries.

How was Welsh society organised?

In some parts of Wales which had fallen under direct English rule the feudal system had been introduced and at the local level the most important figure in society was the Lord of the Manor. In the rest of Wales the princes had previously acted as the local landlords, deciding who farmed what land and how much tax they should pay. However, after the conquest of 1282–83 the position of the prince acting as Lord of the Manor was taken over by the **uchelwyr**

▲ Monasteries became important in the economic life of Wales. The monks farmed the land, growing crops and rearing sheep. This provided work for many lay brothers

(noblemen or squires). The position of the uchelwyr became increasingly important in Welsh society after 1300.

The estate of the uchelwyr was worked by their tenants. There were two types of tenant – the freemen (gwŷr rhydd) and the bondmen (taeogion). The freemen had the right to hunt, ride and to fight in battle. The bondmen lived a hard life. They could not leave their area without permission and they had to produce food for the uchelwyr and the freemen. However, their situation was to change following the impact of the Black Death in 1349.

uchelwyr

freemen

bondmen

◀ Uchelwyr, freemen and bondmen

51

What was the Welsh economy like in 1300?

The Welsh tended not to live in towns but in small farmstead settlements that were scattered over the landscape. They were farmers and their houses had a timber frame, the gaps between the beams being filled in with **wattle and daub**. The house had a thatched roof but no chimney. On some occasions houses were built of stone. The whole family helped to farm the land and manage the animals. They all joined in the annual cycle of ploughing, sowing, reaping, threshing and gathering firewood. They used oxen to pull the ploughs and carts, and **coracles** to fish on the rivers.

Source 4

Tending sheep
Barn used to store food
House of the farmer and his family
Tending cattle
Cow shed
Stable
Threshing
Stockade
Reaping
Collecting firewood
Sowing
Ploughing

▲ An artist's impression of a Welsh farmstead, around 1300

Towns had emerged in Wales by 1300 but they were borough towns, attached to the castles built by Edward I or the Marcher Lords. Towns such as Brecon, Caerphilly, Conwy, Denbigh and Harlech had been granted charters to attract English burgesses to settle there. The burgesses were merchants who lived inside the borough towns and who had been granted special privileges to trade. Welsh people were only allowed to enter the towns on the days of fairs.

There were lots of different trades found within the towns, such as the potter, the smith, the baker, the butcher, the saddler. When the Welsh rose up in rebellion under the leadership of Owain Glyndŵr in 1400 (see page 61) these towns became the main focus of the Welsh attacks.

Source 5

[The bed] is placed along one wall of the house and is stuffed only with a few thin rushes, while its only covering is a stiff coarse blanket, which they weave locally and call a brychan. Everyone goes to bed fully clothed … a fire is kept burning all night at their feet.

From Gerald of Wales' *Description of Wales*, 1194

How did the Welsh live their daily lives?

According to the monk Gerald of Wales, the Welsh wore only a thin cloak over a shirt, leaving their feet and legs bare. They slept in those same clothes, in a common bed made of rushes. They took great care with looking after their teeth and in cutting their hair regularly. They had only a single meal in the evening. Their diet consisted of a combination of meat, fish, oats and dairy produce, washed down with ale or cider. They did not use tables or chairs but sat on the floor to eat, using their fingers to pick up food from bowls and platters placed on rushes.

How important was Welsh culture and tradition?

The bards or poets were very important in Welsh society and they always received a warm welcome in the houses they visited. They brought with them the latest news and they would entertain the household with songs, poetry and stories. In times of war and hardship they played a big part in keeping up the spirits of the people by singing about the brave deeds of their princes. Periodically they competed against each other in Eisteddfod, such as the one held by Lord Rhys in Cardigan in 1176 (see page 37).

Before 1282 the best bards and poets lived in the Llys or court of the Welsh princes but after the downfall of the house of Gwynedd (see page 44) the protectors of the bards were the wealthy freemen, the uchelwyr. They were substantial landowners, proud of their ancient families. The bards sang in praise of these noblemen and in return they were given food and shelter in their **plas** or great hall. After 1282 the plas rather than the Llys became the centre of bardic **patronage**.

▲ How the Welsh dressed, according to Gerald of Wales

Source 6

The whole population lives almost entirely on oats and the produce of their herds, milk, cheese and butter. They eat plenty of meat, but little bread.

From Gerald of Wales' *Description of Wales*, 1194

▲ A bard/poet on his journey between the houses of the uchelwyr

---

ACTIVITIES

1 Look at your completed diagram from the activity on page 50. Form yourselves into groups of six. Take it in turns to explain to the rest of the group the bullet points you have listed in the segments of the diagram. Allow the others time to add any points they have missed in their diagram.

2 Use Source 4 and your own knowledge to:

   a) write a job description for a Welsh tenant farmer living in the year 1300 (refer to all the different jobs that will have to be undertaken on the farm)

   b) write a description of the living facilities available to the new tenant (refer to what the house looks like outside and inside).

Extension task

3 Sources 5 and 6 come from Gerald of Wales' book, *Description of Wales*, which he wrote in 1194. How useful is the work of Gerald to a historian researching what life was like in Wales in the fourteenth century? (Use the diagram on page 8 'Questions to ask when examining a source' to help you.)

4.2 **What economic and social changes affected Wales during the fourteenth century?**

Historians often refer to the fourteenth century as a 'period of crisis' in Wales because it saw major social and economic changes, and changes in the structure of Welsh society. You are now going to investigate what events caused this period of crisis and how the impact of those events changed life in Wales.

What events caused the 'period of crisis'?

Period of famine and bad harvests before 1349

Sudden climate change at the start of the fourteenth century led to colder and wetter weather. Bad harvests between 1315 and 1317 caused severe famine which continued into the 1320s. Cattle were also affected by plagues which reduced their numbers. Severe weather caused farmland around the village of Newborough on Anglesey to disappear under sand dunes following a violent storm in 1330. The entire town of Kenfig in Glamorgan was also buried under sand dunes.

The arrival of the Great Pestilence or Black Death

In the middle of the fourteenth century, a plague known as the Black Death killed between a half and a third of Europe's population. The plague began in central Asia and made its way into Europe, reaching England in 1348. By 1349 it had reached Wales, with terrible consequences.

Starting in the south east, the Black Death spread across Wales in 1349, causing catastrophe. Historians believe that over a third of the population (around 100,000 people) died as a result of the plague. The north seemed to be more badly affected than the south. At Deganwy in Caernarfonshire all the bondmen died, and at Nantconwy there were 147 bondmen before the plague but only 47 afterwards. Ruthin in Denbighshire was particularly badly hit (see Source 4) and in the lordship of Dyffryn Clwyd, 139 died within a fortnight. In the diocese of Hereford, 43 per cent of the priests died during 1349–50.

Source 3

The plague took the lives of my gentle darlings … Handsome Ieuan was taken nine years before the others; and now the worst turn of all has happened, … Morfudd was taken, fair Dafydd was taken, Ieuan, everyone's cheery favourite, was taken, with an unceasing lament Dyddgu was taken, and I was left, feeling betrayed and stunned …

The bard Llywelyn Fychan describes the death of his children during the plague

Source 1

For Wales, as for most of Europe, the fourteenth century may be described as a period of crisis. By the end of the thirteenth century the steadily increasing population had outstripped the amount of land which could be brought into cultivation. This was accompanied by a deterioration in the climate; colder and wetter weather now meant poorer harvests and a greater risk of famine.

A. D. Carr, *Medieval Wales*, 1995

Source 2

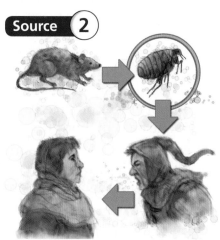

▲ How plague was spread. Fleas living on rats bit people. Infection resulted in bubonic plague – swellings (or buboes) of glands – or plague affecting the lungs (pneumonic), which was caught through breathing in germs from an infected person

Source 4

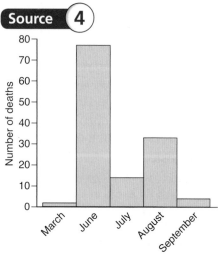

▲ Graph showing the number of deaths from the plague in Ruthin town

The economic and social consequences of the Black Death

The sharp fall in population caused plough land to be neglected and farmsteads to be abandoned. Many bondmen died and could not be replaced, so there was a severe shortage of labour. Those bondmen who did survive could now demand freedom and payment for their jobs, which they had previously done for nothing. Trade declined sharply, prices fell but taxes increased. Some villages became abandoned because everyone had died or moved on. To add to the feeling of despair and insecurity, further outbreaks of the plague occurred in 1361–62, 1369, 1379 and 1391.

Source 5

Before   After

▲ How the Black Death affected economic and social relations between landowners and workers

Source 6

Those bondmen who had survived seized the opportunity to remove the chains which had bound them to the land. They abandoned holdings. Tenancies became vacant, unharvested crops were left to rot, and mills and fisheries fell into ruin. Such events resulted in an end of the old feudal order and led to much greater social mobility.

G. H. Jenkins, *A Concise History of Wales*, 2007

ACTIVITIES

1 What evidence can you find to support the view that the years 1300 to 1350 were a time of 'crisis' for people living in Wales? Use the following sub-headings to help structure your answer:

- The weather
- Illness and disease
- Changes in population levels
- Number of deaths

2 In pairs, work out whether the coming of the Black Death made life better or worse for those Welsh farmers who survived the spread of this disease. Divide your work into two columns, one headed 'Better', the other headed 'Worse'. (Use Sources 5 and 6 as well as your own knowledge.)

Extension task

3 Use the internet to research:

a) the symptoms of the Black Death, and

b) the differences between the bubonic and pneumonic plagues.

The growing frustration in Wales about English rule

> As there were now fewer tenants, English officials saw a sharp decline in the money they received from the population. To compensate for this, the officials raised their rents and taxes. This put more pressure on the people who were left, who now had to make up the same amount in taxes that the officials had received before 1349. Many of these officials acted harshly and were dishonest.

> The start of the Hundred Years War in 1337 meant that many Welshmen like Dafydd Gam and Matthew Goch were forced into doing military service in the King's army in France. As many Welshmen were skilled archers these longbowmen were in great demand and they played an important part in bringing about victory in the Battle of Crécy. However, these costly battles resulted in heavier taxes which put an added burden on the Welsh population. When these former soldiers returned they found it difficult to adjust to civilian life and this resulted in increased public disorder.

Background
The Hundred Years War
This was a series of wars fought, on and off, between England and France from 1337 to 1453. It started when King Edward III of England made a claim for the throne of France. He wanted to protect his lands in south west France and also to protect the valuable wool trade between English merchants and the weavers of Flanders. Despite several important victories such as the Battle of Crécy in 1346, by 1453 the English had been almost completely driven out of France. The Hundred Years War was over.

▼ An illustration showing the siege of Montagne in 1378. The Welshman Owain Lawgoch (Owain the Red Hand) is seen dying with an arrow in his chest. He fought in the Hundred Years War on the side of the French against the English forces. He was assassinated by an Englishman named John Lamb

> The uchelwyr were no longer allowed to run their estates according to Welsh law.

> Welsh traders were denied the trading rights granted to English burgesses living in the borough towns.

> Well qualified and educated Welshmen were increasingly being passed over and not promoted to the top jobs in the Church in Wales. These posts were given to English churchmen. No Welshman was appointed Bishop of Llandaff between 1323–1566 or Bishop of St David's between 1389–1496.

Source 7

With all these tensions at every level of society, Wales in the last decade of the fourteenth century was ready for an explosion and that explosion came in 1400 with the Glyndŵr Rebellion.

A. D. Carr, *Medieval Wales*, 1995

Conclusion

By the end of the fourteenth century there was growing tension and frustration in every level of Welsh society. A combination of social, economic and political problems resulted in the outbreak of a major rebellion against English rule in 1400.

ACTIVITIES

1 Imagine you kept a diary during the first half of the fourteenth century. Write entries for each of the following years, describing the key events:

1315   1320   1330   1348
  1349   1350   1361

2 Why were so many Welsh people increasingly complaining about English rule after 1350? (In your answer you should refer to the following groups: tenants, soldiers, traders, the uchelwyr and parish priests.)

3 In pairs, think about what factors were most important in bringing about change in the fourteenth century. Arrange the factors below in order of importance, with the most important first. Give reasons for your choices.

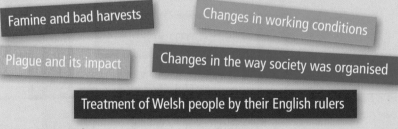

Famine and bad harvests

Changes in working conditions

Plague and its impact

Changes in the way society was organised

Treatment of Welsh people by their English rulers

Extension tasks

4 'A period of crisis'. Do you think this is an accurate description of life in Wales during the fourteenth century? Explain your answer.

5 Think of some other captions to describe life in Wales during the fourteenth century.

REVIEWING YOUR INVESTIGATION

a) How many of the questions that you asked at the start of this investigation (see page 49) have been answered so far?

b) Think of some other questions that you would now like to ask to further your investigation.

4.3 **What were the main religious changes that affected Wales after 1300?**

From 1100 to 1300 there had been a rapid growth of monasteries across Wales. There were the Benedictine 'black' monks who built monasteries close to Norman castles, and the Cistercian 'white' monks who built their monasteries in isolated locations. The monks of both religious orders followed a strict lifestyle laid down by St Benedict in the sixth century. What was it like being a monk in Wales in the fourteenth century, and how far had that lifestyle changed by the end of the fifteenth century?

What was daily life like for the monks living in the monasteries of Wales in the fourteenth century?

Source 1

▲ Map showing the spread of Cistercian monasteries across Wales. The year of their foundation is given in brackets

I'm a monk of the Cistercian order. I have to follow the strict rules made in the sixth century which make sure I devote my life to God and helping others. I like the simple lifestyle.

I live in a monastery. Each monastery follows the same basic plan. The church is built of finely worked stone and is in the shape of a cross. The church is the main feature of the monastery. Next to it is the cloister, a covered walkway around an open square. From this run off a series of rooms which include a chapter house for reading, a kitchen and refectory, and the monks' dormitories upstairs.

Source 2

Live as poor people

Do not marry or have sexual relations

Look after the poor, the sick and the old

Give food and shelter to travellers

Eat simply and wear simple, rough clothes

Copy out precious manuscripts

▲ The rules of St Benedict

Source 3

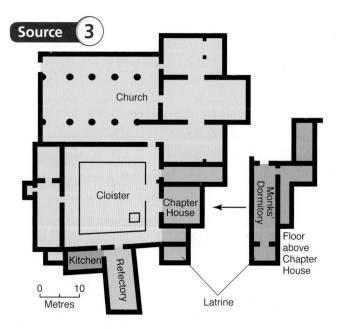

▲ The plan of Valle Crucis Abbey in Llangollen. This plan was typical of most Cistercian monasteries in Wales

My typical day starts at 2a.m. with Matins service. We have seven services throughout the day. Each has a different Latin name depending on the time of day. We finish with Compline at 8p.m. We do get breaks for meals and work.

2a.m.	Prayers in church (Matins)
3a.m.	Return to bed
6a.m.	Prayers in church (Prime)
6.30a.m.	Breakfast in the refectory
7a.m.	Meeting in the chapter house to organise work for the day
8a.m.	Walk in the cloisters
9a.m.	Prayers in church (Tierce)
11a.m.	Main meal in the refectory
12noon	Prayers in church (Sext)
1p.m.	Work
3p.m.	Prayers in church (Nones)
4p.m.	Work
6p.m.	Prayers in church (Vespers)
7p.m.	Supper in the refectory
8p.m.	Prayers in church (Compline)
9p.m.	Bedtime

Our monastery has other important functions in society.

▲ An artist's impression of the monks at prayer in the main church of Valle Crucis Abbey

In my monastery there are two types of monks, the choir monks and the lay brothers. The choir monks mostly pray and study, only doing a small amount of manual work. They have a strict rule of silence and only talk during services. I'm a lay brother. I wear brown robes and work the farms and granges, growing crops, tending cattle and farming sheep. Our monastery is an important part of the economy.

Guardians of knowledge – in our scriptorium (library) we copy old manuscripts and keep a diary of important events.

Treating the sick – in our monastery we have our own hospital. We take care of the sick using our knowledge of herbal remedies.

Other functions of the monastery

Charity work – we take care of the poor, providing them with food and clothes, and looking after them in old age.

Safe haven for pilgrims and travellers – we provide visitors with a free meal and a bed for the night.

ACTIVITY

Work in pairs to prepare an interview with a medieval monk from the 1300s about his typical day. One of you should be the interviewer and work out the questions you are going to ask. The other is the monk and should prepare the answers to the questions. Once you have prepared, present your interview to the rest of the class.

Was there a decline in monastic life by the end of the fifteenth century?

By the late fifteenth century the monasteries were in decline. Gifts of land brought in much more rent money and economic developments such as sheep farming helped to make individual monasteries very wealthy. As monks enjoyed higher standards of living they found it increasingly hard to follow the strict rules of St Benedict. Some monks became greedy and lazy in their daily lifestyle, while others got married and had children. Others were accused of gambling and playing dice.

Settlements had built up outside the monasteries which had resulted in commercial activity such as taverns and stalls selling bread, beer and other goods. These acted as distractions to the secluded lifestyle of the Cistercian order. A Cistercian brother from the 1130s would have found a considerable amount of change had he been able to revisit the monastery in the late fifteenth century.

> **Source** **4**
>
> The Cistercians have many coats, the Welsh none; they have boots and shoes, the Welsh go barefoot.
>
> The medieval writer Walter Map of Herefordshire, commenting on the monks living in the Welsh Marches in the thirteenth century

> **Source** **5**
>
> 1401: We found among other things that some of the monks of your said house bring into their cells private persons from outside, entertaining them … and they live loosely, going out of bounds without leave of the prior.
>
> A comment made following the visit of the Bishop of St David's to the Abbey of Carmarthen in 1401

> **Source** **6**

◀ A fifteenth century manuscript illustration showing a monk being punished in the stocks. He had broken the code of St Benedict

ACTIVITIES

1 Work in groups of four or six and divide into two teams. Take five minutes to gather evidence to prepare your argument: one group has to argue that monasteries performed very useful functions in the fifteenth century; the other group should argue the opposite, that the religious life of monks had become corrupt and the monasteries were no longer doing a good job.

Extension task

2 What evidence is there in Sources 4–6 to show that the standards of monastic life laid down by St Benedict (see Source 2) were no longer closely followed in monasteries in Wales by the late fifteenth century?

REVIEWING YOUR INVESTIGATION

a) How many of the questions you asked at the start of this investigation (see page 49) have now been answered?

b) Think of some other questions that you would now like to ask to further your investigation.

4.4 Owain Glyndŵr: great nationalist hero or rebel leader?

On pages 61–63 read about Owain Glyndŵr, what caused him to rebel against royal authority and his plan to create an independent Wales – and find out what happened when his plan failed.

Who was Owain Glyndŵr?

Curriculum Vitae

- Born around 1359 in the Dee Valley near Llangollen.
- Of princely birth: descended from princes of northern Powys on father's side and rulers of Deheubarth on mother's side. Connections with princely line of Gwynedd.
- Studied law at Westminster before becoming a soldier.
- Fought in King Richard II's army at the Battle of Berwick in 1385.
- Inherited estate at Sycharth and settled down. Sycharth was a typical estate consisting of a great hall, guest house, gate house, dovecot, fishpond, rabbit warren, heronry, mill and parkland.

Why did Owain Glyndŵr rise up in rebellion in 1400?

In 1400 Reginald Grey, Marcher Lord of Dyffryn Clwyd, laid claim to some of Owain Glyndŵr's land. Glyndŵr petitioned the king but he sided with Lord Grey.

The tension increased when Lord Grey deliberately held back a letter from King Henry IV calling upon Glyndŵr to fight in the royal army in Scotland. Lord Grey used this event to convince the king that the Welsh lord was a traitor. The king then declared Glyndŵr's lands forfeit and gave them to Lord Grey. This was the final straw for Glyndŵr.

Owain Glyndŵr: nationalist leader or rebel fighter?

On 16 September 1400 Glyndŵr's friends gathered at Glyndyfrdwy and proclaimed him Prince of Wales. They then attacked and burnt the town of Ruthin, the centre of Lord Grey's power. In the following days they attacked the English strongholds at Denbigh, Rhuddlan, Flint, Hawarden and Oswestry. It was said that the revolt 'spread like fire in a dry season'.

Background

In the 1390s King Richard II was involved in a long-running battle with some of his powerful barons. In 1399 Henry of Bolingbroke returned from exile; he gathered a large body of supporters and took Richard prisoner. Richard was forced to **abdicate** and Bolingbroke succeeded him as King Henry IV. Henry now had to fight off rebellions in England to secure his position as king, which left him with less time to deal with growing problems within Wales.

Source 1

That October (1401), with the whole of North Wales, Ceredigion and Powys siding with him, Owain Glyndŵr fiercely attacked with fire and sword the English living in those parts together with their towns … Because of this the English invaded those parts with a powerful force, plundering and destroying with fire, famine and sword, leaving them a wilderness without sparing neither child nor church.

A report by Adam of Usk, a contemporary chronicler, describing the fierceness of the fighting by both Welsh and English forces

ACTIVITY

1 Give three reasons why Owain Glyndŵr launched his rebellion in the year 1400.

From 1400 to 1403 Glyndŵr won battles against the English forces and the revolt became a national movement. By 1404 Glyndŵr controlled most of Wales and he planned to create an independent Wales free from English authority.

How Glyndŵr planned to create an independent Wales

He created his own 'Great Seal' as a sign that he had law-making power.

He signed a friendship alliance with King Charles IV of France. Charles promised to help the Welsh in their fight against Henry IV. In the summer of 1405 a force of 600 French crossbowmen landed at Milford Haven.

He signed an alliance with Edmund Mortimer and the Earl of Northumberland, powerful English lords who were rebelling against Henry IV. Through the terms of the **Tripartite Indenture** they planned to divide Henry's lands between them.

He called together **Welsh parliaments** at Harlech, Machynlleth and Dolgellau.

He entered into negotiations with Pope Benedict XIII at Avignon, to discuss setting up an **independent Church of Wales**. He planned to create an Archbishop of St David's, breaking Wales free from the Archbishop of Canterbury. Glyndŵr did make sure that only churchmen who could speak Welsh were appointed in Wales.

He planned to set up two **universities** – one in north Wales and one in south Wales. These would train Welshmen to become priests.

Source 2

▲ Glyndŵr's 'Great Seal'

Why did Glyndŵr fail to win independence for Wales?

Much of what Glyndŵr had planned failed to become reality. By 1406 the tide had begun to turn against him and historians have identified a number of reasons for this.

After 1412 Glyndŵr vanishes from history and he is thought to have died around 1415. The place of his burial is unknown.

By 1406 most French soldiers had returned to France.

The rebelling English lords died: the Earl of Northumberland was killed in battle in 1408 and Edmund Mortimer died in a siege in 1409.

By 1412 Glyndŵr was no longer a ruling prince but a fugitive and an outlaw on the run. When Prince Henry became king in 1413 he offered Glyndŵr a pardon but he declined it.

Henry IV and the royal House of Lancaster had grown more powerful – young Prince Henry (future Henry V) was an able military commander and won battles against Welsh forces.

Gradually Glyndŵr lost control over regions of Wales; Anglesey yielded to the King's authority by the end of 1408.

During 1408–09 Prince Henry re-captured Aberystwyth and Harlech castles from the Welsh. At Harlech he captured Glyndŵr's wife and daughters.

What were the effects of the Glyndŵr rebellion?

Many settlements across Wales were destroyed during the rebellion and many lives were lost. Due to the great destruction of crops, buildings and cattle, people could not pay their rents and suffered economic hardship. The country took many years to recover from the effects of the rebellion. King Henry V attempted to stop any future rebellions by imposing harsh punishments upon the Welsh people; these were listed in the Penal Laws (see Source 3).

Source **3**

Welshmen are forbidden from holding land in the borough towns.

Welshmen cannot serve as officials of the king or hold jobs in local government.

Welshmen must not carry weapons.

No Welsh person can marry an English person.

The Welsh must not gather together in large crowds without special permission.

▲ Some of the Penal Laws

Source **4**

The rebellion was more devastating in its course than even the Black Death had been. Owing to the revolt land remained uncultivated, homesteads were destroyed and tenants abandoned their farms. The anger of the rebels had fallen particularly on the hated towns, many of which were left badly damaged.

David Williams, *A Short History of Modern Wales*, 1951

Source **5**

The revolt of Owain Glyndŵr resulted in the widespread destruction of towns and villages, and caused farm land to go to waste. It was at least a generation before most of the areas caught up in the revolt got back to working life. There had been great loss of life and a serious weakening of the economic life of Wales.

From a website produced by the BBC on major historical figures

ACTIVITIES

2 Some historians see Owain Glyndŵr as a nationalist hero while others see him as a rebel leader.

   a) Use the information on pages 61–63 to find examples of Glyndŵr acting as a nationalist hero and as a rebel leader. Copy and complete the chart below to record your findings.

Nationalist hero	Rebel leader

   b) Which of the two descriptions – 'nationalist hero' or 'rebel leader' – do you think better describes Owain Glyndŵr? Remember to support your decision with evidence.

3 Working in pairs, identify reasons why the Glyndŵr rebellion ended in failure. Rank your reasons in order of importance.

Extension task

4 How useful is Source 5 to a historian studying the impact of the Glyndŵr rebellion upon life in Wales? (Use the diagram on page 8 'Questions to ask when examining a source' to help you.)

Nationalist – a person who loves their country and wants it to be independent, not ruled by another country.

Rebel – a person who tries to overthrow a ruler by force, ignoring the law.

4.5 Why was there support in Wales for royal authority by the end of the fifteenth century?

In 1400 the Welsh had risen up in rebellion against the authority of the king of England. Eighty-five years later the Welsh helped a part-Welshman, Henry Tudor, to become the new king of England. What had caused this dramatic shift in loyalty?

What was Henry Tudor's relationship with Wales?

The Tudors from Penmynydd on Anglesey were an ancient Welsh family. They proved to be fierce supporters of Glyndŵr during his rebellion (see pages 61–63) but, after that event, adjusted to the reality of English rule. Henry Tudor's grandfather, Owen, served as a page in the court of Henry V. He later married King Henry's widow, Catherine de Valois, by whom he had two sons – Edmund and Jasper.

Edmund married Margaret Beaufort and they had one child, a son called Henry, born in 1457. As Edmund died before Henry was born, the young heir to the Lancastrian claim to the English crown was brought up by his uncle, Jasper, the Earl of Pembroke, in South Wales. The constant threat of being captured by the Yorkists meant that after 1461 Henry was forced to spend the next fourteen years in exile in Brittany, making only occasional secret visits back to Wales.

Why did Henry Tudor decide to launch his challenge against Richard III in Wales?

Wales was the centre of Henry Tudor's power base. While they were in exile, his uncle Jasper had kept in contact with the leading Welsh nobles, making Wales a safe place to land. On 7 August 1485 Henry and Jasper landed at Dale in Pembrokeshire with 2000 men, mostly Frenchmen. They travelled north to Cardigan and then followed the coast to Aberystwyth, before turning inland towards England. Using the 'Red Dragon' as his standard, Henry's forces were joined by men led by Rhys ap Thomas of Dinefwr, William ap Gruffudd of Penrhyn and Richard ap Hywel of Mostyn.

> **Background**
>
> Between 1455 and 1485 the Lancastrians (Red Rose) and the Yorkists (White Rose) – fought each other for the right to rule England in the Wars of the Roses. In 1483 the Yorkist leader Richard III became king but his murder of his two nephews – the true heirs to the throne – made his rule unpopular and many powerful nobles began to look towards the exiled Lancastrian claimant as an alternative to Richard. The leader of the Lancastrian cause was the part-Welshman, Henry Tudor. In August 1485 Henry fought Richard III for the right to be the next king of England.
>
>
> ▲ The standard carried by Henry on his march to Bosworth
>
> Henry's victory led to the start of the Tudor dynasty.

> **Source** ①
>
> Born and bred in Wales and partly of Welsh origin, Henry set great store by his alleged descent from the ancient Welsh king, Cadwaladr … Before landing in Wales in his bid for the crown he appealed to his fellow Welshmen to join him. Many of them responded eagerly and helped him decisively in achieving his victory.
>
> Glanmor Williams, *Henry Tudor and Wales*, 1985

How important were the Welsh forces in securing Henry's victory at Bosworth?

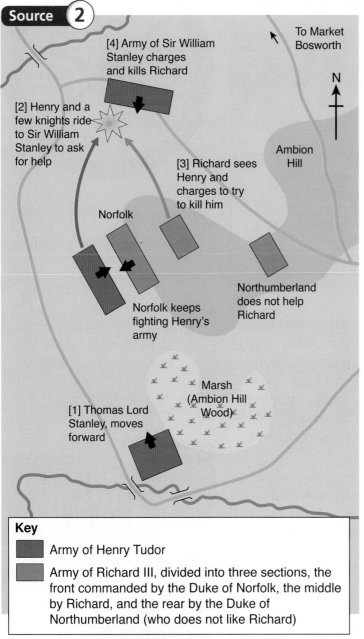

Source 2

[4] Army of Sir William Stanley charges and kills Richard

To Market Bosworth

N

[2] Henry and a few knights ride to Sir William Stanley to ask for help

Ambion Hill

[3] Richard sees Henry and charges to try to kill him

Norfolk

Northumberland does not help Richard

Norfolk keeps fighting Henry's army

Marsh (Ambion Hill Wood)

[1] Thomas Lord Stanley, moves forward

Key

■ Army of Henry Tudor

■ Army of Richard III, divided into three sections, the front commanded by the Duke of Norfolk, the middle by Richard, and the rear by the Duke of Northumberland (who does not like Richard)

◀ Map of the battlefield at Bosworth

By 22 August Henry's army of 5000 men reached Market Bosworth near Leicester. It was there that they met the forces of King Richard III whose army numbered between 10,000 and 12,000 men. Yet there were not two armies at Bosworth but three! As the battle was about to start an army of 8000 men took up position on the northern and southern edges of the battlefield (points 1 and 4 on the map). It belonged to the two Stanley brothers, Thomas, Lord Stanley who had married Henry's mother Margaret Beaufort, and Sir William Stanley. Most of Sir William's army was made up of men from his estates in Flintshire and Cheshire.

If Henry was to secure victory he needed the support of the Stanley's. As he rode out to appeal to Sir William [2], Richard broke from the main body of his army and gave chase [3]. Sir William ordered his men to attack Richard and in the process the king was surrounded, dragged from his horse and killed [4]. Richard's crown was now placed on Henry's head making him the new king – Henry Vll. He became the first Tudor monarch.

Source 3

The battle of Bosworth Field is an important landmark in British history. For England it meant the end of the bloodshed of the Wars of the Roses and the restoration of law and order under the rule of Henry VII. For Wales it meant more. It realised the hopes and dreams of the Welsh people for a prince of their own blood. A new period opens in Welsh history with the accession of the Tudors. The bitterness which had existed for so long between England and Wales was soon to result in the union of the two countries.

Idris Jones, *Modern Welsh History*, 1960

ACTIVITIES

1 In pairs, draw up a list of three reasons to support Henry Tudor's claim that he was partly of Welsh origin.

2 You have been asked by one of Henry's officials to write up a report for the new Tudor king, describing the part played by his Welsh forces in helping to secure victory in the Battle of Bosworth. Use information from pages 64–65.

Extension task

3 Who do you think contributed most to Henry's victory, his Welsh supporters or the Stanley brothers? Give reasons to support your answer.

4.6 How far did the victory of Henry Tudor result in a new beginning for Wales?

When Henry Tudor became king of England in 1485, he also changed life in Wales. Read pages 66–67 to investigate what developments were made: political, religious, economic, cultural and social. To what extent was this the start of a 'new' Wales?

Diagram: a wheel with "Wales in 1500" at the centre and segments labelled: Control of Wales, Work and jobs, Structure of society, Daily life, Religious life, Welsh culture and tradition

Source 1

… the Moses who delivered us from bondage.

The sixteenth century Pembrokeshire historian, George Owen of Henllys, describing Henry Tudor

Source 2

The fifteenth century began with a massive national revolt; it ended with a dynasty of Welsh connections on the throne and a new self-confidence.

A. D. Carr, *Medieval Wales*, 1995

Political developments

Henry rewarded those Welsh leaders who had supported him at Bosworth. His uncle, Jasper, was made Earl of Bedford and Rhys ap Thomas was knighted and later appointed Justiciar of south Wales. Many other Welshmen were rewarded with lesser posts and for the first time in over a century Welshmen were appointed as sheriffs in north Wales. Many of those Welshmen who left Wales and followed Henry to London obtained posts in government.

Religious developments

While the monasteries continued their decline, there was a revival of the Church itself. Many churches were rebuilt, such as St John's in Cardiff. The magnificent churches of Wrexham, Mold and Gresford in north east Wales were rebuilt using money donated by Henry's mother, Margaret Beaufort. Welshmen now also began to be appointed as bishops.

Economic developments

The late fifteenth century saw the first signs of economic recovery. The sharp decline in bondmen following the plague outbreaks caused much land to be given over to grazing. There was an increase in sheep farming, outside of the control of the monasteries. This led to a growth of the wool and cloth industries. The increased wealth helped pay for the rebuilding of many churches. Ports also grew busier due to developing trade with English ports, Ireland and the continent.

ACTIVITIES

1 Your task is to create a snapshot of what life was like in Wales in the year 1500.

   a) Draw a larger version of the diagram above.

   b) Now use the information on pages 66–67 to list four bullet points in each segment to describe the key features under that heading.

Source 3

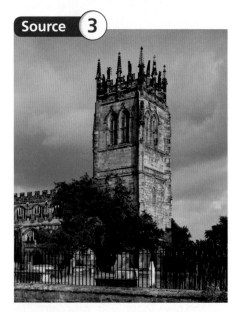

▲ Gresford church was rebuilt in the late fifteenth century and is said to be one of the finest parish churches in Wales

Source 4

◀ The new wing built in the 1460s for William Herbert at his castle at Raglan

Source 5

The Wales of the uchelwyr rapidly took shape in north and south Wales … Towns, manors, professions became less English. The ports of the south, followed by those of the north, became much busier. The families that were to govern Wales for the next 300 years began to emerge, such as the Salisburys, the Bulkeleys, the Vaughans, the Gruffydds, the Dynefors and the Herbert family.

A description of Wales at the end of the fifteenth century by the historian Gwyn A. Williams

Cultural developments

The period 1450–1550 saw the golden age of the Welsh bards and Welsh poetry. Poets such as Guto'r Glyn, Lewis Glyn Cothi and Tudur Aled sang the praises of their uchelwyr patrons, and composed poetry on all aspects of Welsh life.

Social developments

The late fifteenth and early sixteenth centuries saw the rise of the Welsh uchelwyr. Their increasing wealth, together with a more settled political climate, caused many of them to build themselves new, grander houses (see Source 4). William Herbert, for example, added a modern wing to his castle at Raglan with large glazed windows, decorated interiors and planned gardens. For the wealthy there were improvements in furniture and in the styles of clothes. For the poor tenant farmers, however, there were few changes and their lifestyle and possessions showed little change from those of their grandparents and great grandparents.

ACTIVITIES

2 Look at your completed diagram from Activity 1. Form yourselves into groups of six. In turns, explain to the rest of the group the bullet points you have listed in the diagram. Allow the others time to add any points they have missed in their diagram.

3 It is the year 1490 and you have just visited the new living quarters built by William Herbert at his castle at Raglan (Source 4). Write a letter to a friend describing what you have seen. You should refer to the new style of building, the furniture (Source 6), the fine clothes worn by the Herberts (Sources 4, 6) and the entertainment you received from the bards.

4 You have been asked by a publisher to design a full-page diagram for inclusion in a new KS3 textbook on Welsh history. The title of your diagram is 'Life in Wales at the start of the reign of Henry Tudor'. You should include pictures and writing, and refer to the types of houses, furniture, fashion, popular activities, the new churches and the new king.

Extension task

5 The year 1485 is often used by historians in Britain to mark the end of the Medieval Period and the beginning of the Early Modern Period. Do you think 1485 marks a dividing line between the old Wales and the beginning of a new Wales? Give reasons to support your answer.

Source 6

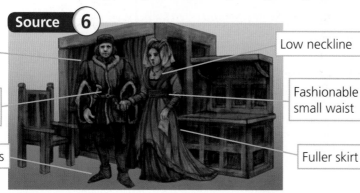

Padded shoulders

Tightly belted waist

Pointed shoes

Low neckline

Fashionable small waist

Fuller skirt

◀ Developments in furniture and clothes by the late fifteenth century

End of section assessment: How far did life in Wales change between 1300 and 1500?

In this section you have examined the major events that helped to shape Wales between 1300 and 1500. Some of these events had a major impact upon how Wales was ruled and how the lives of the ordinary people living in Wales changed. Other events had little impact and life went on virtually unchanged.

Create a PowerPoint presentation to show how far life in Wales changed over the course of two centuries. To do this you will need to compare the key features of 1300 and 1500, following the structure below.

Use the following headings for each slide and follow the bullet points to identify change/continuity between 1300 and 1500. You can use the information you wrote in the wheel diagram activities on pages 50 and 66 to help you.

History skills targeted

 Historical knowledge and understanding

 History enquiry

 Organisation and communication

1: How was Wales governed?
Factors to consider:
- Welsh princes
- Marcher Lords
- King of England
- Rebellion

2: How was society organised?
- Structure of society
- English settlements
- Welsh settlements
- Types of houses/buildings

3: How did the economy operate?
- Welsh farmsteads
- English boroughs

4: What religious developments took place?
- The Norman church
- Monks and monasteries

5: Welsh custom and tradition
- Changes in the patronage of the bards
- The importance in Welsh society of customs and tradition

6: How did the Welsh live their daily lives?
- Style of houses
- Types of furniture
- Types of clothes
- Manners and customs

7: Four causes of change
Identify four causes of change in the period 1300 to 1500 and rank them in order of most important to least important. Write a sentence to explain each of the causes and give two reasons why your first choice was the most important change.

REFLECTION AND REVIEW:

Now that you have completed your investigation into how events between 1300 and 1500 shaped Wales you need to reflect upon your learning. How many of the questions you thought up on pages 49 and 60 have you now answered?

If you were going to study this unit again think about what you would do differently and the different types of questions you would ask. Copy and complete the triangle below to help you reflect upon and review what you have learnt in studying this unit.

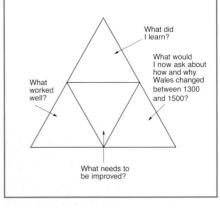

Glossary

abdicate   give up or resign position as king

bailiff   a medieval manor official appointed by the lord

bard   professional Welsh poet and minstrel

Benedictine   order of monks founded by St Benedict in the sixth century; they wore black robes

biased   taking sides, being one-sided

borough   a town that had a charter

burgess   a town dweller who had special rights

chamberlain   an official in charge of the household of the king or noble

charter   a document granting special rights

chronology   placing events into the right order according to date and time

Cistercian   order of monks founded at Citeau in France in 1098; they wore white robes

common land   land open to all people

coracle   small boat made of wickerwork, covered with hide

coronation   the crowning of a monarch

curtain walls   the walls surrounding a castle

diocese   a church district that is the responsibility of a bishop

dues in kind   paying taxes in goods instead of using money

earldom   land held by an earl

Eisteddfod   a Welsh cultural festival devoted to poetry, literature and music

Englishry   an area in Wales that had been settled by the English and was ruled according to English law

evidence   sources of information – written, oral or physical – that helps the historian come to conclusions

fact   thing or event known to have happened

fallow   land on which no crops are growing

garrison   soldiers guarding a castle

homage   showing respect to and promising to obey an overlord

independent Church of Wales   outside the control of the Bishop of Canterbury and the Church of England

interpretation   explaining the meaning of something

Justiciar   the king's representative in Wales

keep   central tower of a castle

Llys   the royal court of a Welsh king or prince

manorial system   the estate of a lord and the responsibilities of the peasants living on it

March of Wales   the area of Wales conquered by individual Norman Marcher lords and held by them from the eleventh to the sixteenth century

Marcher Lords   Norman lords who settled on the border between England and Wales, obtaining land by pushing into Wales by conquest

motte and bailey   a castle on a mound (motte) and with a courtyard (bailey)

opinion   a belief or point of view

overlordship   the authority of a king, prince or lord over his tenants

palisade   a fence of wooden stakes surrounding early castles

patronage   having the support of somebody important or influential

pitched battles   where two armies face each other and engage in battle

plas   the mansion of a Welsh lord

primary evidence   sources which were made or written at the time the events happened

Principality   the part of Wales that was ruled by the King of England

secondary evidence   something written or produced after the event, by someone who was not there

serf   an ordinary person in the Middle Ages who was forced to work on the land

sheriff   a local official who kept law and order

source   a document or authority from which information is obtained

taxes   the compulsory payment of money on property, income and goods purchased

Tripartite Indenture   the planned division of Wales and England into three regions

uchelwyr   Welsh landowners who became the leaders in their community and the patrons of the bards

university   a place of learning

wattle and daub   twigs woven together with mud and straw

Welsh parliament   a Welsh assembly having law-making powers

Welshry   areas of Wales where Welsh people lived and which were ruled according to Welsh law

Index

Answers to Activity 1, page 4

Physical = A, E, F, G, I

Visual = C, J, K

Written = B, D, H, L

Answers to Activity 4, page 7

9 = Roundhouse, The Iron Age

10 = Houses for Industrial Workers, Nineteenth Century

11 = Modern Housing, Twenty-First Century

12 = Rich Landowner's House, Eighteenth Century

13 = Elizabethan Town House, Tudor Period

14 = Castle of Edward I, Medieval Period